First Edition

ISBN Numbers:

(Ebook) — 978-1-965551-19-6

(Paperback) — 978-1-965551-20-2

(Hardcopy) — 978-1-965551-21-9

(Workbook) — 978-1-965551-24-0

A Note to the Reader

This book was not written from a place of solved wisdom. It was written from beside you, from the specific, unglamorous experience of loving someone completely and watching, in quiet devastation, as the relationship strains under the weight of that love. From the exhaustion of a parent who has given everything and is still, somehow, losing ground. If you have found this book, you are probably somewhere in that experience right now. And that you are here, that you chose, at whatever hour this is, to reach toward something different rather than simply carry what you're carrying back to bed matters more than you may currently believe.

Three things before you begin.

The distance growing between you and your child is not a verdict on your love. It is a response to its expression. That distinction is the entire foundation of what follows, and it is worth holding from the very first page.

Everything in this book is a tool, not a test. The practices ahead are not measures of whether you are good enough. They are instruments— precise, practical, and built from genuine research and real parenting experience. There is no grade at the end.

You do not have to read this book perfectly to benefit from it. Read it the way you would read something written by a trusted friend who has been where you are. Put it down when you need to. Pick it up when you're ready.

The only thing this book asks of you is honesty. Not the performed version, but the authentic version. The kind that looks at a hard truth without immediately reaching for a more comfortable framing. That honesty is already available to you. You have shown it in the love that refuses to stop trying, even when the trying has been producing the wrong results. These practices are not designed for ideal conditions. They are designed for the parent who is tired, who is scared, who may navigate this alone, and who is choosing to do the work, anyway. If that is you, this book was written for you specifically.

The relationship you are imagining is not a fantasy. It is a destination. And the distance between where you are tonight and where that destination is, is smaller than your fear is currently telling you.

Turn the page.

Contents

Part I: Unmasking — VIII

Introduction: The Parent Who Found This Book Tonight — IX

1. The Grip That Feels Like Love — 1

2. The Walls We Inherited — 8

3. The Hidden Grief Nobody Talks About — 16

4. The Cost You Haven't Fully Added Up — 23

5. A Journey, a Map, and a Compass — 31

6. Five Walls, Five Doorways — 40

7. See It Clearly — 46

8. Own It Completely — 54

9. Release The Grip — 64

10. Hear What They're Actually Saying — 73

11. Step Into The Life You Were Building Toward — 82

12. When Nothing Seems to Be Working — 92

13. The Co-Parent Conversation — 102

14. Loving the Adult Child You Didn't Expect — 112

15. The Teenager Who Won't Talk to You — 122

16. Reclaiming the Parent You Always Meant to Be — 132

17. When It's Working — What to Do Next — 142

18. The Relationship You Were Always Building Toward — 152

19. Conclusion: The Open Hand Is the Strongest Hold — 160

20. Appendices   167

21. References   183

22. Reader Review Requests   188

Part I: Unmasking

Before anything can change, it must be seen. Part I is not about fixing — it is about illuminating. In these five chapters, you'll name the pattern, trace its roots, grieve what it has cost, and arrive, finally, at a map and a compass for the journey ahead. Nothing asked of you here is more than honest. And honesty is everything.

Introduction: The Parent Who Found This Book Tonight

There is a particular quiet that fills a house after a hard night, and if you're holding this book right now, you know exactly what that quiet sounds like. Maybe something was said that can't be unsaid. Maybe a door closed and didn't reopen. Maybe nothing dramatic happened at all, just another evening where the conversation stayed on the surface, where you tried and felt the distance anyway, where you watched your child move through the room and felt, with a hollow ache you couldn't quite name, that you were losing them. Not to anything you could point to. Just... losing them. So here you are. It's late. The house is still. And somewhere between the events of tonight and the hope that something can change, you found this book.

I want you to know something before we go any further: you have been seen. Not because I can read your mind, and not because your situation is identical to every other parent who has found these pages at this hour. But because the particular combination of love and fear and exhaustion and grief you're carrying right now is one of the most universal and least talked-about experiences in modern parenting, this book was written to address it.

The Parent This Book Was Written For. You love your child. That isn't the question, and it never has been. You love them with the full force of everything you are. You have sacrificed for them; you've never once tallied. You have lain awake worrying about them in ways that would exhaust a person half your age. You have rearranged your life, your priorities, and your identity around getting this right.

Despite that, the distance is growing. That's the thing nobody prepares you for. Not the parenting books. Not the well-meaning advice from friends. Not the podcasts. Nobody tells you it's entirely possible to love your child completely, try relentlessly, and still watch the relationship strain under the weight of everything you're doing for them. Nobody hands you a map for the specific, devastating experience of trying harder and getting further away.

Here's what I want you to understand before a single framework has been offered and before you've read a single chapter: **the distance between you and your child is not a verdict on how much you love them.** It is a response, a direct, readable, entirely understandable response, to how that love has been expressing itself.

That distinction is everything. It is, in fact, the foundation on which this entire book is built. You are not a terrible parent. You are a loving parent whose love has been filtered through fear. And that filter, not your love, not your effort, not your devotion, is what's creating the distance you're so desperate to close.

What Fear-Driven Love Actually Looks Like

Fear-driven love is subtle. It doesn't announce itself. It disguises itself as care, as involvement, as the attentiveness that exemplary parents are supposed to have. It looks like the follow-up text sent an hour after your child said they'd be fine. It looks like the question asked not out of curiosity but because the silence has become unbearable. It looks like the rewritten essay, the one you told yourself you were just *helping* with. It looks like the plan quietly amended, the decision gently redirected, the consequence softened because watching them struggle feels, in your body, like a fire-alarm emergency.

None of these things come from a bad place. Every single one of them comes from love. But your child, the one on the receiving end of all this love, doesn't experience it as love. They experience it as a message. And the message, received over and over across months and years, is: *I don't trust you to handle this. I don't believe you're capable. I need to be involved because without me, something will go wrong.* That message builds walls. Slowly, invisibly, and with the best of intentions, it builds walls. And one day you look up and the walls are there, solid and real, and you're on one side of them wondering how on earth they got so high.

The Truth This Book Is Built On

Before we go any further, I want to plant a single truth at the very beginning of this journey. I want you to carry it into every chapter, every exercise, and every difficult moment of honest self-reflection that lies ahead. Here it is:

"The love that lasts in any relationship is always the love that does not demand to be held."

Read that again. Let it settle. The love that *lasts,* not the love that feels most intense, not the love that expresses itself most loudly, not the love that works hardest, but the love that *lasts*. The love that a child grows up carrying with them. The love that becomes the relationship they choose rather than the relationship they tolerate. The love that, twenty years from now, is the reason they call. That love is not built through proximity. It's not built through management. It's not built through a thousand interventions that keep the world at bay. It's built through trust. Through the slow, consistent, often frightening act of opening your hands and allowing your child to become who they were always meant to be, with you beside them, not ahead of them. That is what this book is about.

Where You Are Right Now

Let me describe you with a precision that might feel uncomfortable. You are a parent who has been running on a specific kind of fear for longer than you'd like to admit. The fear looks different from the outside; it looks like involvement, like dedication, like being present, but from the inside, it feels like a low hum of anxiety that never fully switches off. A constant background calculation of what could go wrong and what you need to do to prevent it. You know, somewhere in the honest part of yourself, that you've been holding too tight. You've probably known it for a while. You might have tried to release the grip before ,told yourself you'd back off, stop checking, let things unfold, and found that within days, sometimes hours, the grip had tightened again without you even noticing.

That's not weakness. That's not failure. That's anxiety operating at full strength in the exact role it was designed to operate in: protecting something you love. The problem isn't that you have anxiety. The problem is that your anxiety has been doing your parenting for you. And this book is going to show you, step by step and with full compassion, exactly how that happened, and exactly how to take the wheel back. You are not here because you're a negligent parent. You're here because you're a good one who is ready to become a wiser one.

The Map You're About to Walk

This book is built around a framework called the **WALLS** System: five stages, one destination, and the clearest possible path from where you are tonight to the relationship you're imagining. Each letter of WALLS is a stage. Each stage is a doorway. And the doorways open in sequence, which means you don't need to know everything at once. You just need to know where you are and what the next step requires.

Here is your map:

W — Witness. See your pattern clearly, honestly, and without shame. This is where we name what's actually been happening — not to indict you, but to give you the most honest possible starting point.

A — Acknowledge. Own the full cost of the pattern, on your child, on the relationship, and on yourself. This is not self-punishment. It is the most liberating thing a parent in your position can do.

L — Loosen. Begin the deliberate, structured practice of releasing the grip, one small, intentional step at a time. This is where theory becomes action.

L — Listen. Build the bridge. Learn to ask without managing, to listen without redirecting, and to create the conditions under which your child begins to move toward you rather than away.

S — Soar. Become the parent you always meant to be, the one whose identity doesn't begin and end at the edge of their child's life, and whose love, offered with open hands, creates the relationship both of you were always capable of.

Five stages. One map. And you're already on it because opening this book was the first step.

What You'll Find Here — and What You Won't

This book will not tell you that your child is fine and that you're overreacting. It will not minimize what you're feeling or rush you past the harder parts of this work with the cheerful optimism that feels good on the page and dissolves before breakfast. It will also not tell you that you've failed, that you've damaged your child beyond repair, or that the distance you've allowed to build is permanent. The research on parent-child relationships is unambiguous on this point: this bond is remarkably resilient. It can be repaired, rebuilt, and transformed at any age and at any stage, including this one.

What you will find here is honest work. Practical tools. Authentic stories from actual parents who have walked this exact path. And a framework assembled with one purpose only: to take you from the parent who is walking on eggshells to the parent whose child chooses to call.

The chapters ahead will ask you to look at things you'd rather not look at. They'll ask you to sit with feelings that have been easier to act on than to feel. They'll ask you to practice new behaviours in the middle of real, live interactions with a person who may not immediately respond in the way you're hoping.

None of that is easy. I will not pretend otherwise. But here's what I know with complete confidence, having worked with parents in exactly your position: it is entirely possible. The relationship you're imagining, the one where your child calls not because they should but because they want to, where the conversations go somewhere real, where Sunday dinner feels like a choice rather than an obligation— that relationship is not a fantasy. It is a destination. And this book is the route.

A Word About How This Book Was Written

This book was not written from above you. It was not assembled by someone who has always had it figured out, looking down at those who don't. It was written from *beside* you, by someone who understands from the inside what it costs to love someone so much that the love becomes its own kind of weight. By someone who has seen, in the real world and in the research and in the hundreds of conversations that informed these pages, what becomes possible when a parent makes the shift from holding on to opening up.

Every practice in this book has been tested. Every framework has been refined. Every story you'll read is true , drawn from actual parents who sat where you're sitting tonight and arrived, through this work, somewhere they couldn't have imagined when they started. You are not alone in this. You never were. And the relationship you're fighting for? It's closer than your fear is currently allowing you to believe.

The One Thing to Hold Before You Turn the Page

Before Chapter 1 begins, before we name the pattern and trace it back to its roots and build the map that will take you through it, I want you to hold one thing. Not a strategy. Not a framework. Just the truth. **The** The love **you have for your child is not the problem.** It has never been the problem. The love is real; it is enormous, and it is exactly what's going to make everything that follows in this book possible.

What we're going to do together, across these chapters, across these weeks of honest, deliberate, compassionate work, is not to change how much you love your child. It's changing the *shape* of that love. From a grip into an open hand. From a wall into a door. From the love that says *I cannot let go because I cannot bear the thought of losing you* to the love that says *I trust you. I believe in you. And I love you enough to let you become exactly who you're meant to be.*

That is the love that lasts.

That is what we're building.

And you've already taken the first step.

In Chapter 1, we begin the work of naming exactly what's been happening — the daily behaviours through which fear has been expressing itself as parenting, the specific pattern that has been building the distance you feel, and the single most liberating thing a parent in your position can do: give it a name. Because the thing you can name, you can change.

And the change starts on the very next page.

Chapter One

The Grip That Feels Like Love

Every parent who has ever tightened their hold on a child has done so because, in that moment, letting go felt indistinguishable from losing them. That sentence is worth sitting with. Because if it landed somewhere true in you, if you felt a flicker of recognition rather than resistance, then what follows in this chapter is going to matter in ways that go well beyond the words on the page. We're not here to dissect your parenting. We're here to illuminate it. There is a significant difference. Dissection implies something has gone wrong and needs to be cut apart. Illumination simply means turning on a light in a room you've been navigating in the dark and discovering that the furniture was never quite where you thought it was.

The light we're turning on in this chapter is this: **the daily behaviours that feel most like love are often the ones doing the most damage.** Not because they come from a bad place. But because they come from fear, and fear, however loving its intentions, is experienced by the child receiving it as something else entirely. Let's look at what that actually means in practice.

1.1 The Everyday Face of Fear-Driven Parenting

Fear-driven parenting doesn't look the way you'd expect. It doesn't look like coldness or indifference or neglect. It looks like the opposite of those things. It looks like a parent who is *everywhere*. It looks like the text message sent at 10:47pm, not because something urgent has happened, but because the silence has stretched past the point of comfort and the anxiety needs somewhere to go. It looks like the question asked not out of genuine curiosity about your child's inner life, but because not knowing feels, in your nervous system, like a threat. It looks like the essay that was *just tidied up a little*. The plan that was *gently steered*. The consequence that was *softened, just this once*, because watching them struggle produces a physical response in you that feels identical to watching them fall.

Here is a list of behaviours that anxiety disguised as love most commonly produces. Read through it slowly, and without judgment, simply notice which one feels familiar:

The follow-up text. Sent not because you genuinely needed a response, but because the silence was unbearable.

The reframed question. Asked not to understand your child, but to check. To monitor. To confirm that nothing has gone wrong.

The softened consequence. The natural result of a decision your child made, quietly removed or reduced because you couldn't tolerate watching them experience it.

The rewritten work. The essay, the application, the email, improved beyond what they'd have produced, under the banner of helping.

The pre-empted problem. The obstacle quietly cleared before they encountered it, so they never had the chance to build the muscle of overcoming it.

The managed friendship. The social situation guided, the invitation prompted, the conflict quietly mediated from behind the scenes.

The filled silence. The rush to speak whenever a conversation pauses, because silence in your child's presence feels like disconnection.

None of these behaviours are monstrous. Every single one of them comes from love. But every single one of them also sends a message, and the message, received consistently over months and years, is the same in every case: *I don't believe you can handle this without me.*

1.2 What Your Child Is Actually Receiving

This is the part that's hardest to hear. So I'm going to ask you to stay with it rather than move past it. Your child is not experiencing your love the way you're offering it. When you send the follow-up text, they don't think: *my parent cares about me deeply.* They think: *my parent doesn't trust me to be okay.* When you soften the consequences, they don't feel protected; they feel managed. When you rewrite the essay, they don't feel supported; they feel subtly told that their own effort wasn't good enough.

Over time, these messages accumulate. They build something. And what they build is not closeness; it is distance with a particular quality to it: the distance of a person who has learned, through repeated experience, that the relationship with their parent requires a certain amount of performance. A certain level of reporting. A certain ongoing surrender of autonomy that, at some point, and this point usually arrives somewhere in adolescence, though it can arrive earlier or later, begins to feel unbearable.

That's when the door starts to close. Not because your child has stopped loving you. But because the version of the relationship they've been offered has, over time, become associated with a loss of self. And every human being, at a certain stage of development, will move away from what diminishes them, even if what's doing the diminishing is love.

Dr Daniel Siegel, one of the most respected researchers in adolescent neuroscience, describes the teenage brain as fundamentally oriented toward one developmental task above all others: the construction of an autonomous identity. The teenager who is managed, monitored, and protected from natural consequences doesn't just find this frustrating. At a neurological level, it conflicts directly with the central project of who they are becoming. The distance isn't defiance. It's development. And it's being accelerated by every well-intentioned intervention that says, *let me handle this for you.*

1.3 The Anxiety Behind the Curtain

Here's what's actually running the show. Beneath every behaviour on the list above is a fear. Not a vague, general unease, but a specific fear with a specific shape. And until that fear is named, it will continue to drive the behaviours that are building the distance you're trying to close.

The follow-up text isn't really about needing a response. It's about the fear that something has happened and you won't know in time. The softened consequence isn't really about kindness. It's about the fear that if your child experiences real failure, something in them, or in the relationship, will break permanently. The rewritten essay isn't really about helping. It's about the fear that if they don't succeed at this, the trajectory you've been quietly holding in your mind will be derailed.

These fears are not irrational. They are the predictable, entirely human responses of a person who loves someone deeply and lives in a world where things do, in fact, go wrong. But here is the critical distinction this entire book rests on: **there is a significant difference between genuine care and unresolved fear.** And the behaviours they produce, while they look identical from the outside, are experienced entirely differently by the child on the receiving end. Genuine care says: *I see you're struggling. I'm here if you need me.* Fear says: *I can see you might struggle. Let me prevent that before it happens.* One builds trust. One erodes it. One says: *I believe in you.* The other says: *I don't.*

1.4 The Fear Audit

The first tool this book offers you is called the **Fear Audit,** and it is the most important thing you'll do before moving to any other chapter. The Fear Audit is a written self-assessment. Not a quiz. Not a checklist. A genuine, private, written examination of your own parenting behaviours and the specific fears underneath them.

Here is how it works.

Step 1: List your ten most frequent interventions. Think about the last two weeks. Think about the moments when you stepped in, spoke up, redirected, softened, checked, or took over. Write the ten most frequent examples. Be specific. Not, *I worry too much,* that's a conclusion, not a behaviour. Write the actual behaviour: *I texted him three times on Friday night. I rewrote the opening paragraph of her personal statement. I called the school about the situation with his friend.* Ten behaviours. As specific as you can make them.

Step 2: Name the fear beneath each one. For each behaviour on your list, ask yourself: *what was I afraid would happen if I didn't do this?* Write the answer down. Again, be specific. Not *I was worried,* write what you were actually worried about. *I was afraid he'd been in an accident and I wouldn't know. I was afraid her application would be rejected, and she'd blame herself. I was afraid that if I didn't get involved, the friendship would end and he'd be isolated.* These are the fears. These are what's actually driving the show.

Step 3: Apply the diagnostic question. This is the question that separates genuine care from unresolved fear. For each behaviour on your list, ask yourself this: **"If I were not afraid right now, would I still do this?"** That's it. That's the whole diagnosis. If the answer is yes, if you'd still send the text, still make the call, still offer the guidance, then the behaviour is coming from genuine care. It belongs in your parenting. Keep it. If the answer is no, if the truth is that without the fear, you wouldn't intervene, then the behaviour is your anxiety parenting your child. And it is that behaviour, specifically and only that behaviour, that this book is asking you to work on. You don't have to change everything. You don't have to become a different person. You just have to learn to tell the difference between the parent you are and the fear that's been speaking in your voice.

1.5 What This Is Not

Before we go any further, let's address the thing that might surface for you right now. This chapter is not an accusation. It is not a verdict. And it is not suggesting that the love you've been offering your child has been worthless or harmful in some fundamental way. What it is saying, clearly and without apology, because you deserve the honest version rather than the comfortable one, is that **anxiety disguised as love is not experienced as love by the person receiving it.** That's not a moral judgment. It's a relational fact. And it's one of the most important facts this book will give you, because it explains, more directly than anything else, why trying harder has been making things worse.

The exhaustion you're feeling? It's real. You have been working extremely hard. The growing distance you're experiencing? It's real, too. And it is not, it has never been, a verdict on your devotion. It is a symptom. A specific, nameable, entirely addressable symptom of a pattern that has a name, a history, and — this is the important part, a solution. You can name it now. And naming it, without shame and with full compassion for the person who built this pattern out of love, is the first and most liberating act available to you.

1.6 The Exhaustion Makes Sense Now

Let's talk about exhaustion for a moment, because it deserves more than a passing m ention.Parenting out of fear is *tiring* in a way that parenting from trust simply isn't. When you're operating from the Closed Hand, the hand that monitors, manages, and intervenes, you are carrying two lives simultaneously. Your own and your child's. You're running two risk assessments at all times: one for your world and one for theirs. You're holding two sets of contingencies, managing two sets of outcomes, and carrying the emotional weight of every stumble they take as though it were a stumble you failed to prevent. That is exhausting. Of course, it is. It was always going to be exhausting. The parent who is slowly letting go, who is learning through the practices in this book to open their hand and trust, doesn't just build a better relationship. They reclaim an enormous amount of energy that has been quietly haemorrhaging into a job that was never actually theirs to do.

Your child's life is not yours to carry. Your job is to walk beside them while they carry it. And the difference between those two things, in terms of the quality of the relationship, the well-being of the parent, and the development of the child, is the difference this entire book creates.

1.7 A Note on What Comes Next

The Fear Audit is your first piece of actual work. Do it before you read Chapter 2. Not because the chapters don't work without it, but because the honesty you bring to that written exercise will change the way you read everything that follows. Write it privately. Write it completely. And when you reach the diagnostic question, " *If I were not afraid right now, would I still do this?",* answer it honestly, even when the honest answer is uncomfortable. Because the parent who can look at their own patterns clearly, without flinching away and without collapsing into shame, is the parent who is already doing the most important thing this book asks of them. They are witnessing. And witnessing, done honestly and with compassion, is where everything changes.

The Fear Audit at a Glance

Step	Action	Key Question
1	List your ten most frequent parenting interventions from the last two weeks	What did I actually do?
2	Identify the specific fear beneath each intervention	What was I afraid would happen?
3	Apply the diagnostic question to each behaviour	If I were not afraid, would I still do this?
Result	Separate genuine care (keep it) from fear-driven behaviour (this is what we work on)	What's mine to change?

Table 1: Showing the Fear Audit at a Glance

Key Takeaway 1

The exhaustion and growing distance are not signs of failure; they are symptoms of a specific, nameable pattern. Naming it without shame and with full compassion is the first and most liberating act of transformation available to you. You are not a bad parent. You are a loving parent whose love has been filtered through fear. And now, for the first time, you can see the filter clearly. That changes everything.

The next chapter takes us deeper, not into what you've been doing, but into why. Because the pattern you've just named didn't begin with you. It was handed to you, shaped by the family you grew up in, the beliefs about love you absorbed before you were old enough to question them, and the specific inherited idea that holding on and loving someone were always the same act. Chapter 2 is where we trace that inheritance back to its roots, not to assign blame, but to find the freedom that only comes from understanding where something began. And that understanding, when it arrives, tends to arrive as relief.

Chapter Two

The Walls We Inherited

The most unsettling moment in any parent's self-reflection is not the moment they recognize their own pattern; it is the moment they recognize whose pattern it actually is. You have probably had a version of this moment already. A flash of recognition, maybe mid-argument, maybe in the quiet afterwards, where you heard your own mother's words coming out of your mouth. Or felt your own father's particular brand of silence operating in your chest. Or noticed, with a jolt that was equal parts clarity and discomfort, that the thing you swore you would never do is exactly what you just did. That moment is not a failure. It is, in fact, the beginning of something.

But before we can talk about what it's the beginning of, we need to talk honestly about how we got here, because the pattern you identified in Chapter 1 did not begin with you. It was handed to you. Carefully, unintentionally, and with complete love, it was shaped by the family you grew up in, the beliefs about love and safety you absorbed before you had the language to question them, and the specific, unexamined equation that your upbringing taught you: **Loving someone and holding on to them are the same act. Letting go is the same as losing them.** That equation is the wall. And this chapter is where we trace it back to its foundation.

2.1 The Family You Parented From

Nobody's parents exist in a vacuum. We all parent from somewhere, from a specific emotional landscape built in childhood, from a set of beliefs about love that were never explicitly taught but were modelled so consistently they became invisible, and from a collection of unresolved experiences that quietly shape every interaction we have with the people we love most.

The family you grew up in taught you what love looks like. Not in words, families rarely teach this in words. They taught it in patterns. In the way conflict was handled or avoided. In the way autonomy was encouraged or discouraged. In the way closeness was expressed, or in the way it was withheld until certain conditions were met. Some of you grew up in families where love was conditional in ways that were never spoken but always felt. Where approval came and went depending on performance, compliance, or mood. Where the message , again, never stated, but always present, was that love had to be earned and could be lost.

Some of you grew up in families where anxiety was the operating system. Where one or both parents lived in a state of low-level fear that expressed itself as vigilance, constant monitoring, pre-emptive problem-solving, a kind of hovering closeness that felt like protection but carried, underneath it, the unspoken message that the world was not safe and you could not be trusted to navigate it alone.

Some of you grew up in families where love was genuine and consistent, but loss was present— a bereavement, a divorce, an absence that taught you, at a formative age, that the people you love can disappear. And that the response to that knowledge is to hold on harder.

None of these family environments is a villain. None of the parents who created them were bad people. They were doing exactly what you are doing now: parenting from the emotional toolkit they were handed, shaped by families who were doing the same thing, generation after generation, each one passing on the same unexamined equations about love and loss and what it means to keep someone safe. This is how walls are built. Not through cruelty. Through inheritance.

2.2 The Promise You Made to Yourself

Most parents who find themselves in the pattern described in Chapter 1 made a promise at some point, sometimes explicitly, sometimes as a private internal vow, that they would do it differently. *I will not be as controlling as my mother was. I will not be as absent as my father was. I will not make my children feel the way I felt.* Sound familiar? Here is the uncomfortable truth about that promise: making it is not the same as keeping it. Not because you're weak or uncommitted, but because the pattern you were trying to move away from was never just a behaviour. It was a belief system. An emotional response. A deeply conditioned way of experiencing love and threat and safety, and you cannot think your way out of a conditioned response. You can only understand it, work with it, and gradually, deliberately, replace it.

The parent who swore they would never repeat their own upbringing and then found themselves doing exactly that is not a hypocrite. They are a human being who encountered the full emotional weight of loving a child, the terror of it, the vulnerability of it, the way it opens you up to a quality of fear that nothing else in adult life quite matches, and found that the only emotional toolkit they had for managing that fear was the one they were handed as a child. You reached for what you knew. Of course, you did. The question is not why it happened. The question is what happens next.

2.3 The Generational Thread

Let's trace this more specifically, because specificity makes this exercise genuinely useful rather than just intellectually interesting. Think about your own parent, the one whose pattern most closely mirrors the one you identified in your Fear Audit. Not to blame them. Not to build a case. Just to see the thread. Ask yourself these questions honestly:

What did love look like in their relationship with you? Was it demonstrative or reserved? Consistent or conditional? Available or earned?

How did they handle your growing independence? Did they encourage it, tolerate it, or subtly resist it? Were there costs, emotional or relational, to your attempts to become your own person?

What happened when things went wrong? Did they help you navigate difficulty, or did they remove the difficulty before you could engage with it? Did they trust your capacity to recover, or did they communicate, through their responses, that failure was catastrophic?

What did you learn from them about what letting go means? Was releasing someone you love associated with trust, or with loss?

Now look at your answers. Because what you'll find, most times, is that the pattern you identified in Chapter 1 is not yours alone. It has a lineage. It has been travelling toward you for a long time, and it has been travelling not because it was ever intended to cause harm, but because nobody in the chain ever had the tools to interrupt it. You now have the tools. That is precisely what makes this moment different from every moment that came before it in your family's history.

2.4 Why This Is Not About Blame?

This needs to be said clearly, because without it, everything in this chapter can be mis used.Tracing your pattern back to your upbringing is not an exercise in building a case against your parents. It is not permission to reframe every difficulty in your adult life as someone else's fault. And it is absolutely not a reason to feel worse about where you are. It is precisely and only an act of compassion toward yourself. Because here is what understanding the origin of a pattern actually does: it removes the shame from it. When you understand that the grip you've been keeping on your child is not a character flaw but a learned response, one that was modelled to you, reinforced in you, and handed to you by people who received it from their own parents, you stop experiencing it as evidence that something is fundamentally wrong with you.

And shame is one of the most powerful barriers to change that exist. The parent who believes their pattern reflects who they are will defend it. The parent who understands their pattern reflects what they learned can choose something different. That is the entire purpose of this chapter. Not to explain away the behaviour, the behaviour still needs to change, and we're going to work on that in the chapters ahead. But to give it a history that makes it understandable. Because the thing you understand, you can compassionately dismantle it. The thing you're ashamed of, you hide. And hidden patterns don't change.

2.5 The Wall Origin Story

The second tool this book offers you is called the **Wall Origin Story,** a guided narrative exercise that traces the roots of your anxiety back to your earliest experiences of love, loss, and the grip that followed. This is a writing exercise. It takes approximately forty-five minutes. You will need privacy, paper or a document, and the willingness to be genuinely honest rather than constructively honest, meaning, write what's actually true rather than the version that reflects well on everyone involved. Here is the structure:

Part 1 — The Family Blueprint. Write for fifteen minutes, uninterrupted, in response to this prompt: *"In the family I grew up in, love looked like ____. Letting go looked like ____. When I showed independence, the response was ____. The belief I absorbed about what it means to keep someone safe was ____."*

Don't edit. Don't self-censor. Don't worry about whether what you're writing reflects well on your parents or fairly represents the full complexity of your upbringing. Just write what's true for the version of you that was a child in that family.

Part 2 — The Moment the Grip Formed. Write for fifteen minutes in response to this prompt:

"The first time I understood that love and holding on were the same thing was ____. The experience that taught me that letting go was the same as losing was ____. After that, the way I loved people changed in the following way: ____."

This part is often harder. It may surface a specific memory, a loss, a disruption, a moment of abandonment, real or felt, that has been quietly shaping your emotional responses ever since. Let it surface. Write it down. The thing that's been driving your behaviour from the shadows loses a significant amount of its power the moment it's written on a page.

Part 3 — The Connection to Now. Write for fifteen minutes in response to this prompt:

"I can see this same pattern operating in my parenting in the following specific ways: ____. The fear underneath it — the one I traced in the Fear Audit — connects back to my history in this way: ____. Understanding where it came from changes the way I see it, because ____."

This last section is where the exercise becomes genuinely useful. Not just emotionally cathartic, though it may well be that too, but practically useful. Because the parent who can draw a clear line from their childhood experience to their current parenting behaviour has something that most parents never develop: a map of their own pattern specific enough to work with.

2.6 What Choosing Differently Actually Requires

Here is something the self-help industry doesn't say often enough: understanding a pattern is not the same as changing it. Insight is necessary. It is not sufficient. You can understand completely where your grip came from, feel genuine compassion for the frightened child who formed it, and trace every thread of the generational inheritance with perfect clarity, and still reach for the phone at 11pm. Still rewrite the essay. Still soften the consequences. Because the pattern isn't stored in your intellect. It's stored in your nervous system. It operates faster than conscious thought. And it will continue to operate that way until it is replaced, not understood, not forgiven, not explained, but replaced, through deliberate, repeated practice, with a unique response.

That is what the rest of this book is for. Understanding, which this chapter offers, is the foundation. It is what makes the work that follows feel like a choice rather than a demand. It is what transforms "I have to stop doing this" into "I understand why I've been doing this, and I am choosing something different" and that shift, from compulsion to agency, is the entire difference between a change that sticks and one that doesn't. You are not your pattern. You are the person who inherited it and is now, for the first time, holding it at a distance close enough to see it clearly. That distance is the beginning of freedom.

2.7 The Inheritance You're Choosing Not to Pass On

There is one more dimension to this chapter, and it is perhaps the most powerful motivator available to you at this stage of the work. Every pattern that goes unexamined gets passed on. Not always in identical form, sometimes the child of an overprotective parent becomes a disengaged one, having swung to the opposite extreme in their own reaction against what they experienced. But the underlying emotional equation, love equals control, letting go equals losing, travels forward until someone stops it.

You can stop it. Not perfectly. Not overnight. But genuinely, deliberately, and with the full understanding of what you're choosing not to hand down to the next generation. Your child is watching you. Not just watching how you parent them, watching how you handle fear. How you respond to the loss of control. Whether you can tolerate uncertainty without immediately moving to eliminate it. Whether you can trust someone you love to manage their own life without your constant supervision.

What you model is what they learn. And what they learn is what they will one day bring to their own relationships , with their partners, their friends, and eventually, their own children. The work you are doing in this book is not just about your relationship with your child. It is about every relationship your child will ever have. It is about the version of love they carry forward into the world, and whether it is love with open hands, or love with the grip still in place. That is what's at stake here. And it is worth every difficult page that follows.

The Wall Origin Story at a Glance

Part	Writing Prompt Focus	Time	What It Reveals
1	The Family Blueprint — what love and letting go looked like in your upbringing	15 mins	The inherited belief system driving your current pattern
2	The Moment the Grip Formed — the experience that fused love with holding on	15 mins	The specific emotional origin of your anxiety response
3	The Connection to Now — how the past is operating in your present parenting	15 mins	The direct line between your history and your behaviour

Table 2: Showing the Wall Origin Story at a Glance

Key Takeaway 2

The walls between parent and child were not built by indifference — they were built by love shaped by fear, passed down through generations. Understanding where the pattern came from is not an excuse for it; it is the act of compassion toward yourself that makes choosing differently genuinely possible. You didn't invent this pattern. You inherited it. And you are the first person in your family line to choose, with full awareness, to put it down. That is not a small thing. In fact, everything.

Chapter 3 asks you to turn toward something that has been sitting just beneath the surface of everything you've read so far, something that has been driving more of the behaviour in Chapter 1 than the anxiety alone, and that almost no parenting book has ever given you language for. It is grief. Not the grief of death or dramatic loss, but the quieter, more persistent grief of a parenting season that is ending. The loss of being needed completely. The loss of the closeness of earlier years. The loss of the family as it once was. It is real; *it is significant, and it has been buried, silently shaping every controlling behaviour this book* dismantles.

In Chapter 3, you'll finally give it a name. And naming it is the single most releasing thing you will do in this entire process.

Chapter Three

The Hidden Grief Nobody Talks About

Somewhere between the toddler who reached for your hand in a car park and the teenager who walks three steps ahead of you now, a loss occurred ,and nobody gave you permission to mourn it. That loss didn't arrive with a funeral, or a diagnosis, or a phone call that changed everything. It arrived in increments. A school year here. A bedroom door closed there. A conversation that used to flow freely and now requires navigation. A Saturday morning that used to begin with small feet padding into your room and now begins with silence and a closed door and the particular ache of a closeness that once existed and has quietly, incrementally, moved further away.

You have been grieving. You may not have known that was the word for it. You may have been calling it anxiety, or frustration, or the vague and persistent sense that something important is slipping through your fingers faster than you can hold it. But underneath those labels, underneath every follow-up text and every softened consequence and every essay rewritten in the small hours, there has been grief. Genuine grief. Significant grief. And almost entirely unacknowledged grief.

This chapter gives it a name. And naming it, fully, honestly, without the apology that accompanies any admission of parental vulnerability, is the single most releasing thing you will do in this entire process.

3.1 The Grief That Has No Funeral

Our culture has a reasonably well-developed language for certain kinds of loss. We know how to hold a parent whose child has died. We know, imperfectly but genuinely, how to sit with someone whose marriage has ended or whose parent has gone. We have rituals for those losses. We have the language of bereavement. We have a social framework that says: this person has lost something real, and they are allowed to grieve it. What we do not have, what is almost entirely absent from the cultural conversation around parenting, is a language for the grief of a child growing up.

And yet it is one of the most universal experiences of parenthood. Every parent who has ever watched their child become more themselves, more independent, more private, more oriented toward their peers and their own inner world than toward the family that raised them, has encountered some version of this loss. The loss of being needed completely. The loss of the particular intimacy of early childhood, when you were the centre of their universe, and they were the centre of yours. The loss of the family as it once was: smaller, closer, contained within the walls of a single house on a Saturday afternoon.

These are real losses. They are not self-indulgent. They are not signs of a parent who loves too much or who can't let go in a healthy way. They are the inevitable and entirely legitimate emotional costs of loving someone who is becoming more themselves. The problem is not that this grief exists. The problem happens when it goes unacknowledged.

3.2 What Buried Grief Does to a Relationship

Grief that is named can be moved through. Grief that is buried drives behaviour. This is one of the most important sentences in this book, and it's worth pausing on it before we continue. When the grief of a child growing up is never acknowledged, never named, never honoured, never allowed its proper place in the emotional landscape of the parents' experience, it doesn't disappear. It goes underground. And underground, it operates in disguise. It presents as anxiety. As control. As the compulsive need to stay close, stay involved, stay informed. As the follow-up text and the softened consequence and the thousand small interventions that feel, from the inside, like love, and that are, from the inside, partly love and partly something else entirely. They are partly mourning.

The parent who hasn't grieved the loss of their child's earlier years isn't just parenting from fear. They are parenting from an open wound that has never been acknowledged as a wound. Every attempt by their child to grow more independent doesn't just trigger anxiety, it reopens the loss. Every closed door, every unanswered text, every preference for a friend's company over the family's is experienced not just as a present-tense rejection but as a compounding of a grief that has no outlet and no name.

This is why the anxiety feels so overwhelming sometimes. Therefore, the grip tightens even when the intellectual part of you knows perfectly well that it should loosen. It's not just fear driving the response. It's grief. And grief, unlike fear, does not respond to logic. It responds to acknowledgements.

3.3 The Losses This Season Has Brought

Let's be specific. Because specificity transforms a vague emotional ache into something you can actually work with. The grief of a child growing up and away is not one loss. It is a collection of losses, arriving at different times and with different weights, and the parent who has never examined them carries them as an undifferentiated mass, a heavy, unnamed thing that sits in the chest and colours everything. Here are some losses most commonly present in this season. Read through them slowly. Notice which one lands:

The loss of being the first call. There was a time when you were the person they came to first, with the skinned knee, the hard day, the excitement that needed sharing immediately. That season ends quietly and without announcement when someone else becomes their first call. Often a friend. Sometimes a partner. And the parent who hasn't grieved this transition experiences every piece of withheld news not as healthy privacy but as a small bereavement.

The loss of being needed completely. The particular intimacy of a child's complete dependence is unlike anything else in adult experience. You were, for a period, everything to them: their safety, their source, their entire world. That kind of being-needed does something to a person. It shapes their sense of purpose and self in ways that are profound and invisible until it begins to withdraw. The parent who hasn't grieved this loss often unconsciously seeks a replacement, creating situations of need rather than allowing their child to show the competence they've actually developed.

The loss of physical closeness. The child who once climbed into your lap, who held your hand without thinking, who fell asleep against your shoulder on long car journeys, that child is still in there somewhere. But they're housed now in a body that has learned to hold its own space, in a person who finds the casual physical closeness of childhood complicated in ways that have nothing to do with their love for you. This loss is rarely spoken about. It is one of the most quietly devastating ones.

The loss of the family as it was. The Saturday mornings. The holiday rituals. The particular texture of family life when the children were small, and the house was full of a specific noise and need. That season has a closing date, and when it closes, something genuinely precious ends. The parent who mourns this is not being sentimental or irrational. They are acknowledging a real and significant loss.

The loss of the version of yourself that you **were in that season.** This one is the least spoken about of all. When a child needs you completely, you have a clarity of purpose that is hard to replicate in any other context. You know who you are and what you're for. The transition out of intensive parenting isn't just the loss of a season with your child — it's a quiet identity crisis that most parents navigate entirely alone, without language for what they're experiencing and without cultural support for the disorientation it produces.

3.4 This Is Not Weakness

Before we go any further, let's address the response that may form somewhere within you right now. The response that says: *This feels self-indulgent. My child is fine. They're just growing up. I shouldn't be grieving something that's supposed to happen.* That response is understandable. It is also, with complete respect, incorrect. The grief of a child growing up is not self-indulgent. It is not a sign of a parent who can't handle healthy development. It is not evidence of poor emotional regulation or excessive attachment or any of the other quietly pathologising labels that get applied to parents, and particularly to mothers, who admit that the transition out of intensive parenting is painful.

It is painful. It was always going to be painful. The fact that it's developmentally appropriate for your child doesn't make it emotionally easy for you. Both things are true simultaneously: your child is doing exactly what they should do, and you are experiencing a genuine loss in the process of watching them do it.

Both truths deserve acknowledgement. The parent who bypasses this grief, who pushes it down under the weight of practicality, or dismisses it as weakness, or medicates it with busyness, doesn't move through it. They carry it. And they carry it right into every interaction with their child, where it operates as the hidden weight beneath every anxious behaviour this book addresses. You are allowed to grieve this. You are, in fact, required to, because the grief that is bypassed doesn't resolve. It drives.

3.5 The Grief Naming Practice

The third tool this book offers you is the **Grief Naming Practice,** a structured written exercise that identifies and articulates each specific loss this season has brought you. The purpose is straightforward: grief that is named can be moved through. Grief that is buried silently continues to drive the controlling behaviours that are building the distance you're trying to close. This exercise has three parts. It takes approximately thirty minutes. As with the Wall Origin Story in Chapter 2, it requires privacy and the commitment to write what's actually true rather than what sounds acceptable.

Part 1 — The Inventory of Losses Write, without filtering or editing, every specific thing you have lost in this season of parenting. Not vague categories, but specific things. Not *I've lost* closeness, but *I've lost the Saturday mornings when she'd come into our bed and we'd all watch television together. I've lost being the person he called when something good happened. I've lost the particular way she used to reach for my hand without thinking.*

Be as specific as possible. The more specific the loss, the more fully the grief can be acknowledged. Generalisations keep grief abstract. Specifics make it real, and genuine grief is the only kind that can be genuinely moved through. Give yourself fifteen minutes for this part. Write until there is nothing left to write.

Part 2 — The Acknowledgements. For each loss on your list, write a single sentence that acknowledges it as a legitimate loss. Not a reframe. Not a silver lining. Not *but I know this is healthy development.* Just acknowledgement."The The loss of Saturday mornings is real, and it deserves to be mourned." "The loss of being his first call is real, and it deserves to be mourned." "The loss of who I was when she needed me completely is real, and it deserves to be mourned." This step feels simple. It is not. It is, for most parents, the step that produces the most emotion, because it is often the first time these losses have been witnessed with any kind of care. Not fixed. Not reframed. Seen. Give yourself ten minutes for this part.

Part 3 — The Separation This last step is the one that makes the practice therapeutically useful rather than simply emotionally cathartic. For each loss on your list, write the answer to this question: *"How has this unacknowledged loss been showing up in my* *parenting behaviour?"* This is where the connection becomes explicit. Where the parent can see, sometimes for the first time, that the follow-up text isn't just anxiety, it's also the grief of no longer being the person they call first. That the softened consequence isn't just fear, it's also the grief of no longer being needed in the way they once were. That the rewritten essay isn't just control, it's also an attempt to stay involved, to stay close, to hold on to a season that has already, quietly, ended. The behaviour doesn't justify the grief. But the grief explains the behaviour. And the parent who understands what is actually driving their responses has something far more useful than willpower: they have insight specific enough to work with. Give yourself five minutes for this part. Then set it down. Don't immediately move to fixing or planning. Just let what you've written be true for a little while.

3.6 What Happens After the Naming

Here is what most parents discover when they complete the Grief Naming Practice with genuine honesty: Relief. Not the relief of having solved something. Not the relief of a strategy deployed, or a problem addressed. The quieter, deeper relief of having finally told the truth about something that has been sitting in the body for a long time without a name.

Grief acknowledged loses its underground authority. It does not disappear; grief of this kind doesn't disappear, and it isn't supposed to. But it moves from the basement to the living room. It becomes a known presence rather than an invisible driver.

And the parent who knows what they're grieving is no longer at the mercy of it in the same way, because they can distinguish, at the moment, between a genuine parenting response and an emotional reaction that belongs not to the present situation but to an older, deeper, unresolved loss. That distinction, made in real time, in the kitchen or the car or the middle of a tough conversation, is one of the most powerful tools available to a parent trying to change their pattern. It is not the end of the grief. It is the beginning of carrying it more honestly. And a grief carried honestly is a grief that no longer has to express itself as control.

The Grief Naming Practice at a Glance

Part	Focus	Time	What It Produces
1	The Inventory — list every specific loss this season has brought	15 mins	A named, specific map of what you've actually been mourning
2	The Acknowledgement — validate each loss as real and legitimate	10 mins	The first genuine witnessing of your own grief, without reframing
3	The Separation — identify how each unacknowledged loss has been driving your behaviour	5 mins	The direct link between your grief and your pattern — specific enough to work with

Table 3: Showing the Grief Naming Practice at a Glance

Key Takeaway 3

The grief of a child growing up and away is real, significant, and almost entirely absent from existing parenting content. A parent who names this grief, fully, honestly, and with compassion, discovers that what they have been calling anxiety is partly mourning, and that mourning, once honoured, releases the grip it has been keeping on the relationship.

You have not been overreacting. You have been under-acknowledging. There is a profound difference.The loss is real. The grief is legitimate. And the parent who finally names it stops needing to express it through control because the thing that needed acknowledgement has at last received it.

Chapter 4 asks you to do something that may feel, initially, like the hardest thing this book asks of you. It asks you to add up the full cost, honestly, completely, and without softening the numbers. Not as punishment. Not as a reason for shame. But as the foundation from which every genuine, lasting change is built. Because the parent who has truly reckoned with what fear-driven parenting has cost, on their child, on the relationship, on their own sense of self, has access to a quality of motivation that no amount of good intention alone can produce.

Regret, fully felt and honestly faced, is not the end of hope. It is the moment hope becomes something you can actually build on. And that building begins on the very next page.

Chapter Four

The Cost You Haven't Fully Added Up

The most honest thing a parent in your position can do is also, paradoxically, the thing that feels most dangerous: look at the full cost of what has been happening, without softening a single number. Not because you deserve to suffer the looking. But because the parent who has genuinely reckoned with what fear-driven parenting has cost on their child, on the relationship, on their own sense of self, on the other people inside this family has access to a quality of motivation that good intentions alone could never produce.

Regret is not the enemy of change. Avoided regret is. The parent who has half-looked at the cost, who has glanced at it, felt the sting, and then quickly redirected toward something more comfortable, carries that half-seen reckoning as a low-level weight that never quite converts into fuel. The parent who looks fully, stays with what they see, and allows the honest weight of it to land has done something that changes everything that follows. They have converted regret from a paralysing force into the most powerful motivational energy available. That conversion is what this chapter is for.

4.1 The Costs We Tend to Look Away From

There is a reason this chapter comes fourth rather than first. The work of Chapters 1, 2, and 3, naming the pattern, understanding its origins, giving language to the grief beneath it, was not preamble. It was preparation. Because the parent who arrives at this chapter having done that work arrives with something that makes an honest cost reckoning possible: they arrive with compassion for themselves already in place. Without that compassion, this chapter would produce shame. And shame, as we'll discuss in a moment, is precisely what this chapter is not about.

With that compassion intact, this chapter produces something entirely different: clarity. And from clarity, agency. And from agency, the irrevocable decision that something is going to change. Let's look at the costs. All of them. Starting with the one that is hardest to face.

4.2 The Cost to Your Child

This is the cost most parents are aware of in the abstract but have never allowed themselves to fully feel in the specific. Your child has been receiving messages. Not the message you intended, not the message of love and care and deep, devoted attention that you have been trying to send. A different message. And that message, received over and over across months and years of interactions shaped by unresolved fear, has left marks.The marks are not permanent. This is important to hold as you read what follows: the research on relational repair is clear and consistent, and we will come back to it many times in the chapters ahead. But the marks are actual, and they deserve to be honestly acknowledged.

The message received around capability: Every time you stepped in before they had the chance to step up; every pre-empted problem, every softened consequence, every obstacle quietly cleared from their path , your child received a message about what you believed they were capable of. That message, at its core, was: *I don't trust you to handle this.* Over time, some children internalize that message. They begin to believe it about themselves. The child who has never been allowed to fail, recover, and discover their own resilience is a child who has been quietly deprived of the most important thing a parent can give them: the experience of their own competence.

The message received around safety: A parent who monitors, tracks, and intervenes constantly communicates, without words, that the world is a dangerous place requiring constant vigilance. Children who grow up inside that communication often develop their own anxiety, not because they inherited it genetically, though that may also be true, but because the environment they were raised in modelled fear as the response to uncertainty. The anxious teenager is sometimes a direct reflection of an anxious parent's unspoken communication about how safe it is to exist in the world independently.

The message received around the relationship. This is perhaps the most painful cost to look at directly. Your child is not experiencing the relationship the way you experience it. What you experience as closeness, they may experience as weight. What you experience as involvement, they may experience as surveillance. What you experience as love, they may experience as conditional availability, an intimacy that comes at the price of compliance, reporting, and the ongoing surrender of the privacy they need in order to become themselves.

The distance that has grown between you is not because your child has stopped loving you. It is, at least in part, because the relationship, as it has been structured, has required them to choose between closeness with you and the development of their own self. And at a certain age, every healthy child will choose themselves. Not because they don't love you. Because they have to.

4.3 The Cost to the Relationship

Beyond the cost to your child individually, there is the cost to the relationship itself, to the particular, irreplaceable bond between the two of you that is the subject of this entire book. Every relationship has a kind of account. Into that account go deposits: the moments of genuine connection, the conversations that went somewhere real, the times when one person felt truly seen and heard by the other. And from that account go withdrawals: the interactions that left someone feeling managed rather than met, monitored rather than trusted, smaller rather than larger for having been in the other person's company.

Fear-driven parenting makes withdrawals at a rate most parents have never tallied. Think about the conversations that have closed down. The moment your child sensed that the question you were asking wasn't genuine curiosity but data-gathering, they shut the door. The moment they brought you something real, and it became, within a few sentences, a lesson or a warning or a redirection toward the outcome you preferred, and they stopped bringing you real things. The moment they learned that honesty with you came at a price, the price of your anxiety, your intervention, your inability to hear difficult information without mobilizing around it, and began to offer you the edited version instead.

These moments accumulate. Each one is small. Together, they have been building the distance you feel. And then there is the specific cost of the conversations that never happened, the ones your child needed to have with you and didn't, because the relational conditions for them had never been built. The questions they took to their friends instead. The fears they carried alone rather than risk the particular quality of attention that your anxiety produces. The moments of genuine vulnerability that were offered once, met with the wrong response, and then never offered again. These are not recoverable moments. They happened, or they didn't, and the ones that didn't are part of the honest cost that belongs in this reckoning.

4.4 The Cost to Yourself

This cost tends to receive the least attention because the parent in your position has become so focused on their child that the question of personal cost barely registers. But it is real, and it belongs in this reckoning as fully as every other cost, because the parent who ignores what this pattern has cost them personally will eventually run out of the internal resources the transformation ahead requires.

The version of yourself you quietly lost inside the role. Somewhere in the years of intensive, fear-driven parenting, many parents lose track of who they are outside that role. The interests that once constituted their identity. The ambitions that existed before the children arrived. The sense of self that isn't defined by how well the parenting is going. When parenting becomes the primary vehicle through which a person experiences purpose, meaning, and identity, the parenting becomes impossible to release. Not because they won't, but because the question underneath every loosening of the grip is: *if I am not managing this, who am I?* That is a question that this book will help you answer. But first, it needs to be named as a cost: the slow erosion of self that happens when one role consumes everything else is a genuine loss, and it deserves to be acknowledged as such.

The toll of living with chronic anxiety. The physical and psychological cost of sustained anxiety is not metaphorical. It is measurable. The parent who has been operating from a state of low-level fear for years, running two risk assessments simultaneously, carrying the weight of their child's life alongside their own, lying awake with the particular quality of 3 am parenting dread, has been paying a physiological price. The exhaustion is not weakness. It is the predictable output of a nervous system that has been asked to run at a level it was never designed to sustain indefinitely.

The relationship with your partner. If you have one, this belongs in the reckoning. Fear-driven parenting rarely stays contained within the parent-child relationship. It bleeds into the co-parenting dynamic, the marital conversation, and the quality of attention and presence available to the partnership. The parent who is consumed by anxiety about their child is often, in the same season, slowly withdrawing from their partner, not through intention but through simple resource depletion. And the partner on the receiving end of that withdrawal, who may not have the language for what has been happening, has been paying a cost, too.

4.5 Guilt and Shame Are Not the Same Thing

Here is a distinction that underpins everything in this chapter, and everything in the book that follows.

Guilt says: I did something that needs to change.

Shame says: I am something that cannot change.

Guilt is productive. Guilt is the appropriate emotional response to having recognised that your behaviour has had a cost on your child, on the relationship, on yourself, and that something different is required. Guilt points forward. Guilt says: *now that I can see this, I can do something about it.* Guilt is the fuel this chapter produces. Shame is the opposite. Shame doesn't point forward. Shame collapses inward. The parent in the grip of shame doesn't move toward change; they either defend themselves against the painful recognition, or they disappear into it, becoming so saturated with self-condemnation that the energy required for actual transformation has nowhere to go.

As you work through the cost inventory that follows, you will encounter both. You will feel guilt, specific, uncomfortable, forward-pointing guilt about specific behaviours and specific costs. Let that guilt be present. It belongs here. It is not something to bypass or soothe away prematurely. And you will probably encounter shame, the voice that takes the specific costs and inflates them into a verdict on who you are as a person and a parent. When you hear that voice, you now have a name for it. And you have the context, built across the first three chapters of this book, to receive it with a unique response:

I understand where this pattern came from. I have named the grief underneath it. I am not my pattern. I am the person who is choosing, right now, to look at it honestly, and that choice is not what a terrible parent does. It is exactly what a good one does.

4.6 The Cost Inventory

The fourth tool this book offers you is the **Cost Inventory,** a private, structured written document that honestly records the specific relational costs of fear-driven parenting across four dimensions.

This is not a punishment exercise. It is a foundation-building exercise. The parent who skips it, or moves through it quickly without genuine honesty, is building the transformation ahead on uncertain ground. The parent who completes it fully is building on bedrock. Here is the structure:

Dimension 1 — The Cost to Your Child

Write, specifically and without softening, how fear-driven parenting has affected your child. Consider their confidence, their developing independence, the messages they have received about their own capability, and how the relationship's dynamics have shaped their behaviour and emotional development. Be specific. Not, *I think it's affected his confidence,* but *I can see that he doesn't try things unless he's certain he'll succeed. He asks me to check everything before he submits it. He has told me, more than once, that he's not good at making decisions.*

Dimension 2 — The Cost to the Relationship

Write the specific ways the dynamic has cost the relationship between you. The conversations that closed. The trust that eroded. The version of your child you don't fully know because the conditions for genuine openness were never built. The specific moments you can identify where a withdrawal was made from the relational account — and the cumulative effect of those withdrawals on where the relationship stands today.

Dimension 3 — The Cost to Yourself

Write honestly about what this pattern has cost you personally. The version of yourself that has been subsumed by the role. The physical and psychological toll of sustained anxiety. The impact on your partnership or marriage. The ambitions, interests, and dimensions of your own identity that have been quietly set aside.

Dimension 4 — The Forward-Facing Reframe

This final dimension is where the inventory converts from reckoning into fuel. For each cost you've identified, complete the following sentence: *"Because I can see this cost clearly, I am now choosing to_____."* This is where regret becomes agency. Not by bypassing the pain of what you've seen, but by allowing it to point somewhere. The cost of inventory is not an indictment. It is the most honest foundation from which genuine, lasting change is built. And this is the truth that sits at the centre of this entire chapter: **We cannot live in the what-could-have-been. We can only build from what can be, and that building starts today, from exactly where you are.**

The Cost Inventory at a Glance

Dimension	Focus	What It Produces
1	The cost to your child — capability, independence, and received messages	Honest clarity about the specific impact on the person you love most
2	The cost to the relationship — closed conversations, eroded trust, missed connection	A clear-eyed account of where the relational account stands today
3	The cost to yourself — identity, anxiety, partnership	Recognition that you are also a person who has paid a price in this pattern
4	The forward-facing reframe — convert each cost into a specific commitment	The precise moment regret becomes motivational fuel rather than paralysing weight

Table 4: Showing the Cost Inventory at a Glance

4.7 The Most Courageous Thing

There is a particular courage required to do what this chapter asks. It is not dramatic courage, not the courage of a grand gesture or a public declaration. It is quieter than that, and harder.

It is the courage to sit with the full, honest weight of something without immediately moving to fix it, explain it, or make it more comfortable. To let the cost be what it is. To resist the instinct to pivot mid-reckoning, to everything you've done right, not because the things you've done right don't matter, but because this exercise requires the complete version rather than the balanced one.

The parent who can do that, who can look fully at the cost, feel the guilt without drowning in shame, and then convert that guilt into the irrevocable decision that something is going to change, has done something that the chapters ahead will ask them to build on. They have laid the most honest and durable foundation available. From this foundation, everything becomes possible. Not easy. But possible. And, possible, it turns out; it is all you need.

Chapter 5 marks the end of Part I and the beginning of something different. The work of Unmasking, naming the pattern, tracing its origins, honouring the grief, and reckoning with the cost, is complete. What follows is not more looking back. What follows is the map forward.

In Chapter 5, you'll meet The Love Without Walls System in full: *the journey, the map, and the compass that will take you from the parent you've been examining across these four chapters to the parent your child is waiting for. You are not lost. There is a proven path. And it begins with a single, clear-eyed step that is already closer than your fear has been allowing you to believe.*

Chapter Five

A Journey, a Map, and a Compass

Every parent who has ever tried to change a deep, long-running pattern without a clear system has discovered the same painful truth: insight without structure is just awareness without traction. You have done significant work in the four chapters behind you. You have named the pattern. You have traced it to its origins. You have given language to the grief beneath it and looked honestly at the cost it has produced. That work was not preamble, it was essential. The parent who arrives at a system without that foundation tends to use the system as a set of techniques to manage a problem they haven't yet fully understood. The parent who arrives here having done the work of Part 1 brings something that techniques alone cannot manufacture: genuine readiness. You are ready. And what you're ready for is this.

5.1 The Problem With Every Other Resource

Before we introduce the system, it's worth being direct about something. There is no shortage of parenting advice. Books, podcasts, therapists, online communities, well-meaning relatives, the volume of guidance available to the parent in your position is, if anything, part of the problem. Not because the advice is wrong. Some of it is genuinely useful. But because advice, on its own, doesn't bridge the gap between knowing and doing.

You already know you should let go more. You already know that hovering isn't helping. You already know, at some level, that the anxiety is driving more of your parenting than the love is. You knew all of that before you opened this book. Knowing has not been the missing ingredient. Structure has.

What the parent in your position has been missing is not more information about what healthy parenting looks like. It is a clear, sequenced, practical system that tells them not just *what* to do but *when* to do it, *how* to do it in the middle of a real interaction with a real person who is not cooperating, and *how to find themselves* on the map when they've lost their footing and need to know what the next step requires. That is what The Love Without Walls System is. And this chapter is where you meet it in full.

5.2 The Three Elements of the System

The Love Without Walls System is built from three elements that work together as a complete architecture. They are not interchangeable. Each one does something that the other two cannot do alone. **The first element is the journey:** the 30-Day Connection Reset, the daily practice structure that converts the system's principles from ideas into habits, one micro-practice at a time, across six weeks of deliberate, structured change.

The second element is the map: The Bond Blueprint, the five-stage WALLS Framework that gives you the complete picture of the transformation journey, shows you exactly where you are within it, and sequences the work in the precise order that the psychology of relational change requires.

The third element is the compass: The Three-Hand Method, the real-time diagnostic tool that you carry into every parenting interaction, every difficult conversation, and every moment when the old pattern reaches for the wheel, and you need a three-second check to put the deliberate choice back in your hands.

Journey. Map. Compass.

You cannot navigate well without all three. The journey without a map is an effort without direction. The map without the compass is knowledge without application. The compass without the journey is a tool you never build the muscle to use. Together, they create a complete system that helps people bridge the gap between knowing what to do and actually doing it, covering broad goals, daily tasks, and immediate decisions. Let's look at each one.

5.3 The Map — The Bond Blueprint and the WALLS Framework

You were introduced to the WALLS Framework in the Introduction. Here, at the close of Part I, you receive it in full, because the parent who understands the complete architecture of the journey before they walk it will navigate the difficult stages with orientation rather than panic.

The WALLS Framework is the five-stage roadmap of The Love Without Walls System. Each stage is a doorway. Each doorway opens in sequence. And each one delivers something the previous stage made possible. Here is the complete map:

W — Witness

What it requires: Clear, honest, compassionate self-observation. The willingness to see your pattern fully, its daily behaviours, its underlying fears, the grief it has been carrying ,without flinching away and without collapsing into shame.

What it delivers: The most honest map of your own pattern that you have ever had. Not a verdict, but a starting point. The parent who completes the Witness stage knows exactly where they are, how they got here, and what they're actually working with. From that clarity, every step that follows becomes navigable. **The tools it uses:** The Fear Audit. The Wall Origin Story. The Grief Naming Practice. The Cost Inventory. You have already completed these. You are already through the Witness stage.

A — Acknowledge

What it requires: Moving from passive recognition to active ownership. Writing the Cost Inventory in full. Distinguishing between the guilt that fuels transformation and the shame that prevents it. And for those navigating this journey within a partnership, beginning the conversation with a spouse or co-parent that introduces the system's language as a shared framework rather than a personal critique.

What it delivers: The precise motivational combination that research identifies as the most powerful forward-moving force available: regret fully felt, paired with agency fully claimed. The parent who completes the Acknowledge stage doesn't just understand what needs to change. They have made the irrevocable internal decision that it is going to.

The tools it uses: The Cost Inventory (Dimension 4 — the forward-facing reframe). The Partner Alignment Conversation framework.

L — Loosen

What it requires: The most practically demanding work of the entire framework. Deploying the Three-Hand Method as a daily operating system. Executing the first Deliberate Step Back, choosing not to intervene in one specific, identified situation and allowing the natural consequences to land. Beginning to build the Evidence File.

What it delivers: The first real neural pathway of deliberate choice. The parent who completes the Loosen stage has done the thing that every previous attempt at change skipped: they have practised the new behaviour in a real, live situation, not in a journal, not in a therapy session, but in the kitchen, in the car, in the middle of the conversation, and discovered that the anxiety they feared would be unbearable was, in fact, survivable.

The tools it uses: The Three-Hand Method. The Deliberate Step Back protocol. The Evidence File.

L — Listen

What it requires: Mastering the Open Question practice. Starting the Repair Conversation. Implementing the Consistency Protocol, the daily, weekly, and monthly practice structure that converts insight into a living habit rather than a temporary adjustment.

What it delivers: The bridge. The child who experiences a parent who asks without managing and listens without redirecting will, almost always and eventually, begin to move toward them. Not immediately. Not dramatically. But the quality of the space between parent and child changes, and the parent who has built this stage can feel the difference, even before the child has articulated it.

The tools it uses: The five Open Question structures. The Repair Conversation framework. The Consistency Protocol.

S — Soar

What it requires: Completing the Identity Reclamation Practice. Defining personal Flourish Markers. Writing The Legacy Letter.

What it delivers: The relationship. Not a repaired version of what existed before, but something better. The parent who reaches the Soar stage and sustains it through the ongoing challenges of real family life has not just changed their parenting. They have become someone different: a person whose identity is full enough that the relationship with their child is the richest thread in a rich fabric rather than the only thread in an empty one. And that person, it turns out, is the parent their child finds most worth returning to.

The tools it uses: The Identity Reclamation Practice. Flourish Markers. The Legacy Letter.

5.4 The Compass — The Three-Hand Method

The WALLS Framework is the map. But a map alone doesn't prevent you from getting lost in the moment — the specific, charged, real-time moment when your teenager says something that sends the anxiety firing, when the silence stretches past the point of comfort, when the old pattern reaches for the wheel before you've even registered what's happening. For those moments, you need a compass. Something small enough to carry in your pocket and fast enough to use before the old response has already landed.

The Three-Hand Method is that compass. It is built on a simple but foundational observation: every parenting interaction, at its core, draws from one of three modes. Not occasionally. Every time. And the mode you're operating from in any moment determines, more than almost anything else, what your child receives from the interaction and what it does to the relationship. The three modes are The Closed Hand, The Open Hand, and The Guiding Hand.

The Closed Hand

The Closed Hand is the mode of fear-driven parenting. It monitors, manages, controls, and intervenes. It steps in before the child has the chance to step up. It asks questions designed to check rather than to connect. It offers help that isn't really help — it is anxiety in the shape of help. The Closed Hand is not malicious. It is frightening. And it produces the distance this book is designed to close.

Most parents operating from the Closed Hand are not aware they are doing so in the moment. The response feels natural, caring, and exactly what a good parent should do. The Three-Hand Method interrupts that automatic response with a three-second check that creates just enough space for a different choice.

The Open Hand

The Open Hand is the mode of trust. It allows. It waits. It asks genuine questions, and then genuinely listens to the answers without redirecting toward a preferred outcome. It tolerates the discomfort of uncertainty because it has learned, through the deliberate practice of the Loosen stage, that its child's capability is real and does not require constant supervision to exist. The Open Hand is not passive. It is not indifferent or disengaged. It is the active, conscious choice to trust rather than control, and in the early stages of this work, it is the hardest choice available. It gets easier. But only through practice.

The Guiding Hand

The Guiding Hand is the mode of mentorship. It is neither the grip of the Closed Hand nor the complete release of the Open Hand. It is the considered, requested, appropriately boundaried involvement of a parent who has been invited in, who offers perspective when asked, who shares wisdom without insisting it be followed, who is present, available, and genuinely useful without being indispensable.

The Guiding Hand is where the relationship ultimately wants to live. It is the mode that most closely resembles the adult friendship this book is building toward: the parent-child relationship in its most mature, most freely chosen, most mutually satisfying form.

The Three-Second Check

In any parenting interaction, a text message received, a conversation beginning, a situation unfolding that triggers the familiar anxiety response, The Three-Hand Method asks three questions in rapid sequence:

1. Name the Hand. Which hand am I reaching for right now? Be honest. The answer is usually obvious within a second if you're willing to look.

2. Check the Driver. What is driving that reach? Is it genuine care — the kind that would still be present if the fear were removed? Or is it anxiety, grief, or a habitual pattern operating faster than conscious thought?

3. Choose the Hand. Given what I've just seen in the last two seconds, is this the hand I want to offer? If not, which hand does this moment actually call for?

Three questions. Three seconds. One deliberate choice. That is the compass. Small enough to carry everywhere. Fast enough to use before the old response has landed. And cumulative in its effect, because every time you run the check and choose differently, you are building the neural pathway of deliberate, trust-based parenting one repetition at a time.

5.5 The Journey — The 30-Day Connection Reset

The map tells you where you're going. The compass tells you which way you're facing. The journey is how you actually get there, not in a single dramatic shift, but through the accumulation of small, daily, deliberate practices that gradually replace the old patterns with new ones.

The 30-Day Connection Reset is the daily practice architecture of Part II. It is a structured sequence of micro-practices, none of which take over ten minutes, that progressively builds the habits of open-handed parenting across six weeks. It does not ask for perfection. It does not require ideal conditions. It asks for one deliberate choice, made one moment at a time, repeated with enough consistency that the new response begins to feel natural rather than effortful.

The research on habit formation is clear: behaviours practised in small, regular increments, with a specific trigger and action, build neural pathways faster and more durably than behaviours attempted in large, infrequent bursts of willpower. The 30-Day Connection Reset is designed around exactly that finding. Ten minutes a day, consistently applied, will produce more lasting change than an occasional hour of intensive effort because it is the consistency, not the intensity, that rewires the pattern.

Each stage of the WALLS Framework has its own set of daily practices within the Reset. As you move through Part II, each chapter will introduce the specific practices that belong to that stage, so you're never working on everything at once, but always working on exactly what the current stage requires.

The Complete System at a Glance

Element	Role	What It Does
The Bond Blueprint / WALLS Framework	The Map	Shows you where you are, where you're going, and what each stage requires
The Three-Hand Method	The Compass	Gives you a real-time diagnostic in every parenting interaction — three seconds, three questions, one deliberate choice
The 30-Day Connection Reset	The Journey	Converts the system's principles into daily habits through structured micro-practices

Table 5: Showing the Complete System at a Glance

Key Takeaway 5

You are not lost. There is a map, a compass, and a proven path. The Love Without Walls System does not ask for perfection or ideal conditions, it asks for one deliberate choice, made one moment at a time, across five stages that will take you from the parent walking on eggshells to the parent your child chooses to call.

The Witness stage is behind you. You have named the pattern, traced its origins, honoured the grief beneath it, and looked honestly at what it has cost. That work is done. What lies ahead is the work of Rewiring, and it begins in Chapter 6 with the full architecture of the WALLS Framework laid out before you like a set of open doorways, each one lit from the other side. You know where you are. You have the map. You have the compass. All that remains is to walk. *Part I is complete. You've done the most important and most demanding work of this book, the honest, compassionate excavation that makes everything that follows possible.*

Part II: REWIRING

Understanding changes what you know. Practice changes what you do. Part II is where the knowing becomes doing — where the insights of Part I are translated, one deliberate choice at a time, into a fundamentally different way of being in the relationship. The stages of the WALLS Framework are walked through in full here, with tools and practices for every step.

Part II begins now. In Chapter 6, you'll receive the complete operational architecture of the WALLS Framework — not just the five stages but the precise sequence in which they open, the specific demands of each one, and the daily practice structure that will carry you through all of them. This is where the work shifts from the parent who knows what needs to change to the parent who is, one deliberate choice at a time, changing it.

The first doorway is already open. Step through.

Chapter Six

Five Walls, Five Doorways

A map is only useful if you understand how to read it before you need it, not when you're already lost and trying to work out which way is north in the middle of a difficult conversation at ten o'clock on a Tuesday night. This chapter is where you learn to read the map. Not in theory. Not as an intellectual exercise. But with the specific, practical fluency that means when you are standing in your kitchen, and your teenager walks past you without a word, and the old pattern fires at full voltage, you know exactly where you are, exactly what the moment is asking of you, and exactly what your next deliberate step requires.

That fluency is what Chapter 6 builds. And it builds it by doing something no chapter before it has done: taking you inside the architecture of the WALLS Framework, not just the five stages, but the precise reason they are sequenced in the order they are, what each stage demands before the next one can open, and how The Three-Hand Method operates as the real-time bridge between the map and the moment.

Part II is called Rewiring. That word was chosen carefully. Rewiring is not the same as deciding. It is not the same as understanding. It is the slow, deliberate, repetition-based process of replacing one neural pathway with another, and it happens not in a single session of insight but in the accumulated quality of a thousand small, deliberate choices made across the weeks and interactions ahead.

This chapter is the orientation before the rewiring begins. Read it carefully. The parent who understands the architecture before walking it will navigate every difficult moment that follows with something that makes all the difference: they will know where they are.

6.1 Why the Sequence Is Not Negotiable?

The five stages of the WALLS Framework are not a menu. They are not five parallel approaches from which you choose the one that feels most relevant to your situation. They are a sequence, and the sequence is not arbitrary. Each stage creates the conditions that make the next stage possible. Skip a stage, or attempt them out of order, and you will encounter the same problem every parent encounters when they try to change a deep pattern without the proper foundation: you will make progress, and then you will relapse, and the relapse will feel like evidence that change isn't possible rather than what it actually is, evidence that a necessary earlier step was skipped. Here is why each stage must precede the one that follows it:

Witness must come before Acknowledge because you cannot genuinely own a cost you haven't fully seen. The parent who moves to Acknowledge without completing Witness produces a Cost Inventory that is intellectually honest but emotionally shallow, a list of things they know they should acknowledge rather than things they have genuinely felt. Shallow acknowledgement produces shallow motivation. And shallow motivation does not survive the difficulty of Loosen.

Acknowledge must come before Loosen because the Loosen stage will ask you to do the most practically uncomfortable thing in this entire framework: to not intervene when every instinct is screaming that you should. The parent who attempts this without having first converted their regret into agency is attempting it on willpower alone. Willpower depletes. Agency, the genuine, felt, internally motivated decision that something is going to change, does not deplete in the same way. It is a unique quality of fuel entirely.

The first "Loosen" must come before "Listen" because a child who has been managed for a long time will not respond to a parent who asks better questions if everything else in the dynamic remains unchanged. The Open Question practice, the heart of the Listen stage, lands differently in a relationship where the parent has already shown, through the Deliberate Step Back, that something has genuinely shifted. Words without behavioural evidence are experienced by the child who has learned not to trust that change is real, as more words. Behaviour first. Questions after.

Listen must come before Soar because the Soar stage asks the parent to invest in their own identity, their own life, their own flourishing, and to do so before the relational bridge has been built risks the child experiencing the parent's self-investment as abandonment or indifference. The parent who has done the Listen stage, who has repaired the conversation, built the daily practice of genuine connection, and created the relational conditions for trust, has earned the right to step back into their own life without the child experiencing it as withdrawal. The sequence protects both parent and child from a misreading that could undo the work of every previous stage.

This is why the sequence is not negotiable. Not because the framework is rigid, but because it reflects something real about how relational change actually happens, and honouring that reality is the difference between a transformation that sticks and one that doesn't.

6.2 The Architecture of Each Doorway

Every stage of the WALLS Framework has the same internal structure. Understanding that structure, before you enter the first doorway, means you will never be disoriented inside a stage, unsure of what it is asking or whether you're doing it correctly. Each stage has four components:

A demand. Something the stage requires you to do, feel, or face that the previous stage has made you ready for. The demand is always specific. It is never vague encouragement to "work on yourself" or "open up more." It is a concrete, nameable action or practice.

A tool. The specific practice or instrument the stage provides for meeting its demand. Every demand in the WALLS Framework comes with its own tool, because a demand without a tool is just pressure, and pressure without direction produces anxiety rather than change.

A discomfort. Something about the stage that will feel difficult, not because the framework is hard, but because genuine change always passes through a moment of discomfort, and the parent who knows what the discomfort of each stage feels like in advance will not mistake it for evidence that they're doing it wrong. They'll recognise it as evidence that they're doing it right.

A delivery. What the stage produces, not as a distant eventual outcome, but as a concrete, identifiable shift that the parent can feel within the stage itself, before moving on to the next one. Every doorway delivers something real before asking you to step through the next one. Here is the complete architecture of all five doorways:

The Complete Doorway System at a Glance

Doorway 1 — Witness

The Demand	See your pattern clearly, honestly, and without shame — its daily behaviours, its underlying fears, the grief beneath it, and the full cost it has produced
The Tools	The Fear Audit. The Wall Origin Story. The Grief Naming Practice. The Cost Inventory
The Discomfort	The temptation to soften what you see — to acknowledge the pattern in broad strokes while avoiding the specific details
The Delivery	A complete, honest, compassionate map of your own pattern — specific enough to work with

Doorway 2 — Acknowledge

The Demand	Move from recognition to ownership. Feel the cost and convert it into the decision to change
The Tools	The Cost Inventory Dimension 4. Partner Alignment Conversation
The Discomfort	The pull toward shame rather than guilt — and refusing that voice
The Delivery	Regret converted into agency and commitment

Doorway 3 — Loosen

The Demand	Release the grip in real interactions
The Tools	Three-Hand Method. Deliberate Step Back. Evidence File
The Discomfort	Anxiety during non-intervention — evidence of growth
The Delivery	Evidence of child capability that accumulates

Doorway 4 — Listen

The Demand	Build connection — ask and listen without control
The Tools	Open Questions. Repair Conversation. Consistency Protocol
The Discomfort	Silence and resisting the urge to fill it
The Delivery	Gradual movement toward connection

Doorway 5 — Soar

The Demand	Become a full individual, not defined only by parenting
The Tools	Identity Reclamation. Flourish Markers. Legacy Letter
The Discomfort	Guilt of self-investment
The Delivery	Authentic adult relationship with your child

Table 6: Showing the complete architecture of all five doorways at a glance

6.3 The Three-Hand Method as the Real-Time Bridge

The WALLS Framework is the architecture of the transformation across weeks and months. The Three-Hand Method is its application in the space of seconds. Every stage of the WALLS Framework has a corresponding Three-Hand orientation, a default mode that the stage is working to build, and a shadow mode that the stage is working to replace. Understanding this correspondence means The Three-Hand Method isn't just a standalone tool; it is the lively expression of wherever you are in the WALLS Framework, moment by moment throughout your day. Here is how the correspondence works:

The Three-Second Check — **Name the Hand, Check the Driver, Choose the Hand** — is the mechanism that makes this progression real in actual interactions rather than only in reflection. It is what bridges the gap between the parent you are becoming across the framework and the parent you are in the specific, charged, real-time moment when the old pattern is the path of least resistance. Use it every time. Not occasionally. Not only when you remember. Every time, because the neural pathway of deliberate choice is built through repetition, not through occasional heroic effort.

6.4 The 30-Day Connection Reset — Daily Practice Architecture

The map tells you where the doorways are. The compass tells you which hand you're reaching for at any moment. The journey, the 30-Day Connection Reset, is the daily structure that moves you through the doorways, one deliberate practice at a time.

Each practice in the Reset takes only ten minutes. Each one is tied to a specific stage of the WALLS Framework. And each one is designed around a fundamental principle of behaviour change that the research consistently supports:

Small actions, consistently repeated, produce more durable change than large actions attempted only occasionally.

The parent who spends ten minutes every day running The Three-Hand Check and logging the hand reached versus the hand chosen will build a more robust new pattern than the parent who spends a full hour once a week reviewing their parenting. Not because the hour is worthless, it isn't, but because the ten daily minutes are happening closer to the actual behaviour they're designed to change. Proximity to the pattern is what produces change in the pattern. Here is the daily practice structure for Part II:

Morning (3 minutes): Set one intention for the day. Which hand do you want to lead with in today's most likely difficult interaction? Name the interaction. Name the hand. Write it down.

At the moment **(3 seconds):** Every significant parenting interaction gets the Three-Second Check. Name the Hand. Check the Driver. Choose the Hand. No logging is required at the moment, just the check.

Evening (7 minutes): Review the day's interactions. Log two things only: the moment you were most tempted by the Closed Hand, and the moment you most successfully chose differently. One line each. No analysis required. The pattern emerges from the log over time. Simple. Repeatable. And cumulatively in ways that will be visible within the first two weeks if you do it consistently.

Key Takeaway 6

The WALLS Framework is not a philosophy. It is a map with doorways, and every doorway opens in sequence. The parent who understands the architecture before beginning the journey will navigate the difficult moments with orientation rather than panic, knowing exactly where they are and what the next step requires.

You now have that understanding. You know the sequence and why it is not negotiable. You know the internal architecture of each stage, its demands, its tools, its discomfort, and its delivery. You know how The Three-Hand Method operates as the live expression of the framework in real time. And you know the daily practice structure that will carry you through the work ahead. The map is in your hands. The compass is in your pocket. The journey begins now.

Chapter 7 takes you into the first working stage of the framework, Witness, and applies it with a precision that goes significantly deeper than the groundwork laid in Part I. You'll conduct the full Fear Audit within the WALLS Framework context, map your ten most frequent interventions to their specific underlying fears, and run The Three-Hand diagnostic in a real interaction for the very first time. Part I showed you the pattern. Chapter 7 shows you exactly where it lives in the specific texture of your daily life, and gives you the first real, practised experience of choosing differently. That first experience changes something. It always does.

Chapter Seven

See It Clearly

W — Witness

The most powerful thing a parent can do at the start of this stage is also the thing that feels least like doing anything at all: stop moving long enough to see what is actually happening. Not what you fear is happening. Not what you hope is happening. Not the version of events that protects you from the hardest parts of the honest picture. What is actually, specifically, measurably happening in your daily interactions, in your habitual responses, in the gap between the parent you intend to be in the morning and the parent you have been by the time the evening arrives?

Witness is the first stage of the WALLS Framework for a reason that goes beyond sequencing. It is first because everything else, every practice, every conversation, every deliberate step back, is only as good as the accuracy of the map it's built on. A vague awareness that you've been holding too tight is not a map. It is a feeling. And feelings, however genuine, do not tell you which specific behaviours to work on, which specific fears are driving them, or which specific moments in your day are most in need of a different response. That precision is what the Witness stage produces. And this chapter is where that precision is built.

7.1 What a Witness Actually Means

There is a version of self-observation that is not witnessing. It is judging. It looks like witnessing; it involves looking at your own behaviour, noticing patterns, and making assessments. But it produces a fundamentally different result, producing clarity and the quiet, energised stillness of a person who finally understands what they're working with. Judging produces shame. And shame, as you now know, is not fuel. It is paralysis wearing the mask of self-awareness.

The Witness stage asks for something specific: the ability to observe your own patterns with the same quality of attention you would offer a good friend describing theirs. Not softened, a good friend deserves honesty, and so do you. Not inflated into evidence of fundamental inadequacy, a good friend's pattern is not who they are, and neither is yours. Seen. Clearly, specifically, and with the compassion that makes the seeing useful rather than merely painful.

This is harder than it sounds. The instinct to either defend or condemn is deeply conditioned, particularly around parenting, where the cultural stakes of being seen as inadequate are unusually high. The parent who can hold the middle ground, seeing clearly without flinching, feeling the discomfort without drowning in it, is developing a capacity that will serve them not just in this stage but across every stage of the framework that follows. That capacity is called self-witnessing. And like every other capacity in this book, it is built through practice.

7.2 The Full Fear Audit — Inside the WALLS Framework

You completed a version of the Fear Audit in Chapter 1. That version introduced you to the concept, to give you an initial, orienting look at the pattern and the fears beneath it.

The Fear Audit you are about to complete is different. It is fuller, more specific, and conducted now within the WALLS Framework context, which means it is not just identifying your pattern. It is mapping it with enough precision to serve as the foundation for everything the Loosen and Listen stages will ask of you. Here is how it works.

Step 1 — The Ten Interventions

Write your ten most frequent parenting interventions from the last two weeks. You have done this before, so this time push for greater specificity than you managed in Chapter 1. Not *I check up on him too much*, that is a conclusion. Write the actual behaviour, in the actual context: *On Wednesday, I texted him four times between 9 pm and midnight, asking if he was home yet. On Thursday, I rewrote the first two paragraphs of her university application because I told myself I was just tightening the language. On Friday, I called the school about the friendship situation, even though she had specifically asked me not to.* Specificity is not self-punishment. Specificity is precision. And precision makes the map workable.

Step 2 — The Fear Beneath Each One

For each of the ten behaviours, write the specific fear that drove it. Not a general category of fear, but the actual, honest, specific fear that was operating in that moment. *I was afraid he was drinking and had lost track of time, and* that something *had happened. I was afraid her application wouldn't be strong enough without the changes, and she'd be rejected, and she'd blame herself, and the rejection would define how she saw her own potential. I was afraid the friendship situation would escalate, and she'd end up isolated, and I wouldn't find out until it had already done damage.*

These are genuine fears. Write them without apology.

Step 3 — The Three-Hand Classification

This is the step that Chapter 1 version did not include. For each behaviour on your list, apply The Three-Hand diagnostic:

Is this the Closed Hand? Is this behaviour driven by anxiety, by unresolved fear, by the grip, and would it stop if the fear were removed?

Is this the Open Hand? Is this behaviour driven by genuine trust, by a real, evidence-based belief in your child's capability and resilience?

Is this the Guiding Hand? Is this behaviour invited mentorship, a response to a genuine request from your child for your perspective or involvement? Be honest. Most of the behaviours on your list will be the Closed Hand. That is expected. That is what the pattern looks like from the inside. The purpose of this classification is not to produce a score but to show you, with complete clarity, which hand has been governing most of your daily parenting interactions.

Step 4 — The Diagnostic Question

For each Closed Hand behaviour on your list, apply the diagnostic question you first encountered in Chapter 1:

"If I were not afraid right now, would I still do this?"

If the answer is no, and for most of the behaviours on your list it will be no, circle that behaviour. These are the specific, named, precisely located instances of the pattern you are working on. Not your parenting. Not who you are as a parent. These specific behaviours, in these specific contexts, driven by these specific fears. That is your map. That is what Witness produces.

7.3 Naming the Grief Within the Witness Stage

The Fear Audit maps the behaviour and the fear. But as you discovered in Chapter 3, not everything driving the Closed Hand is fear in the straightforward sense. Some of it is grief, the unacknowledged mourning of a parenting season that is ending, operating underground and expressing itself as control.

Within the Witness stage, grief naming is not a separate exercise. It is an extension of the Fear Audit, a second layer of honesty applied to the same list of behaviours. For each Closed Hand behaviour you have circled, ask a second question alongside the diagnostic one:

"Is there a loss underneath this behaviour, something I mourn that **this intervention is trying, unconsciously, to hold on to?"**

Take the example of the parent who rewrites their child's university application. The fear beneath it might be: *I'm afraid the application won't be strong enough.* But the grief beneath it might be: *I am terrified that this application is the last thing I will ever write with her, that this is the end of a season of involvement in her life that I am not ready to lose.*

Both are true simultaneously. The fear is genuine. The grief is equally real. And the parent who can name both has a significantly more honest and complete map of what is actually driving the behaviour, which means they have a significantly more targeted and effective approach to changing it. Go back through your circled behaviours. For each one, write one sentence beneath the fear: *"The grief underneath this is____."* Not every behaviour will have a grief layer. Some are straightforward anxiety without a mourning dimension. But many will. And the ones that do are often the ones that have been most resistant to previous attempts at change, because they were being addressed only at the level of the fear, while the grief beneath them continued to drive.

7.4 The Three-Hand Diagnostic in a Real Interaction

Everything so far in this chapter has been reflective work — done in writing, in private, at a remove from the live interactions that are the actual terrain of the change you're making. It is time to close that gap. The last practice of the Witness stage is to apply the Three-Hand Method in a real interaction. Not a reconstructed one. Not a hypothetical. A live, actual, present-tense parenting interaction, the next one that presents itself after you finish reading this page. Here is how to approach it.

Choosing the Interaction

For your first live application of The Three-Hand Check, choose a low-stakes interaction. Not the conversation you've been dreading for three weeks. Not the topic that reliably produces your highest-anxiety response. Choose something ordinary — a text message you're about to send, a question you're about to ask, a situation you're about to step into that doesn't carry the full emotional weight of the most difficult dimensions of your relationship.

The reason for starting low-stakes is not avoidance. It is neural pathway building. The Three-Second Check is a skill. Like every skill, it is easier to learn in conditions that aren't fully charged, and it is easier to transfer to high-stakes situations once it has been practised in lower-stakes ones. Start small. Build the pathway. The high-stakes moments will come, and when they do, you'll have something more than good intentions to bring to them.

Running the Check

At the moment, before you send the text, before you ask, before you step into the situation:

1. Name the Hand. Which hand am I reaching for right now? Take one honest second and name it. Closed, Open, or Guiding.

2. Check the Driver. What is driving that reach? Fear? Genuine care? Unresolved grief? The habit of the pattern operating faster than thought? Name the driver specifically, not as a judgment, but as information.

3. Choose the Hand. Given what I've just seen, is this the hand I want to offer? If yes, proceed. If no, pause. Take one breath. Choose differently.

Three steps. Three seconds. One choice. After the Interaction, the reflection. Once the interaction has ended, write three sentences in your daily log:

"The hand I initially reached for was _____."

"The hand I chose was _____."

"The gap between those two — or the absence of a gap — tells me _____."

That third sentence is the one that builds awareness over time. Because the parent who tracks not just which hand they reached for but what the reach felt like, how automatic it was, how much resistance the deliberate choice required, whether the anxiety rose or stayed manageable, is building a self-knowledge that grows more precise with every entry.

The neural pathway of deliberate choice is not built in a single use of the Three-Second Check. It is built in the twentieth century. The fiftieth. The one hundred and twenty-third. Each repetition lays down a slightly more established alternative to the default. Each one makes the next deliberate choice marginally less effortful than the last.

This is how rewiring actually happens. Not in a breakthrough moment. In an accumulation of small, consistent, logged, deliberate choices that gradually become the new default.

7.5 What the Witness Stage Delivers

When the Witness stage is complete, when the Fear Audit has been done in full, the grief layer has been identified beneath each relevant behaviour, and the Three-Hand Check has been applied in at least one live interaction, the parent has something they have never had before.Not a resolution. Not a transformation. Something more immediately useful than either of those things:

A map. A specific, honest, compassionate, personally calibrated map of exactly where they are. Which behaviours are driven by fear? Which fears are driving them? Which losses are operating beneath the fear? Which hand has been governing most of their parenting interactions? And from that first live application of The Three-Hand Check, the first small, irrefutable, entirely personal piece of evidence that a different choice is likely.Not comfortable. Difficult. But possible. And, possibility, as this book has been saying since the Introduction, is all you need.

7.6 A Note on What Witness Is Not

The Witness stage is not a permanent residence. It is a doorway, and doorways are walked through, not lived in. Some parents, particularly those with a strong tendency toward self-reflection and introspection, are tempted to extend the Witness stage indefinitely. To keep refining the map, keep adding detail, keep examining the pattern, because as long as they're examining it, they're not yet required to change it. This is a sophisticated form of avoidance. It looks like diligence. It feels thorough. And it is the Closed Hand applied to the process of transformation itself, gripping the safety of reflection rather than stepping through into the discomfort of deliberate change.

The map you have built in this chapter is precise enough. It does not need to be perfect before you proceed. The Acknowledge stage, the next doorway, is where the map gets used, not where it gets refined further.

When you have completed the Fear Audit in full, named the grief layer beneath each relevant behaviour, and applied The Three-Hand Check in at least one live interaction, you are ready. Not because everything is resolved. Because the Witness stage has done what it was designed to do. You can see where you are. That is enough to take the next step.

The Witness Stage at a Glance

Practice	What It Requires	What It Produces
The Full Fear Audit	Ten specific behaviours, the fear beneath each, Three-Hand classification, diagnostic question applied	A precise, named, personally calibrated map of the pattern
Grief Layer Identification	A second question applied to each Closed Hand behaviour: what loss is underneath this?	The complete picture—fear and grief both named, both workable
First Live Three-Hand Check	One real, low-stakes interaction with the Three-Second Check applied and logged	The first neural pathway of deliberate choice—small, real, and irrefutable

Table 7: Showing the Witness Stage at a Glance

Key Takeaway 7

Witnessing is not judgment; it is illumination. The parent who completes this stage arrives at something they have never had before: a clear, honest, compassionate map of exactly where they are, how they got here, and why none of it makes them a negligent parent. It makes them human. And from this map, every subsequent step becomes possible.

You are not judging yourself. You are seeing yourself perhaps for the first time, with the accuracy and the compassion that genuine change requires. That is not a minor act. It is, in fact, the act that makes every other act possible.

The next stage of the WALLS Framework asks you to move from seeing to owning, from the clear, honest map you have just built to the irrevocable internal decision that what you've seen on that map is going to change. Chapter 8 is the Acknowledge stage, and it will ask you to do something that the Witness stage has, quietly and carefully, been preparing you for: to feel the full weight of the cost without being crushed by it, and to let that weight become the most powerful fuel available for the transformation ahead. The map is in your hands. Now it is time to decide what you are going to do with it.

Chapter Eight

Own It Completely

A — Acknowledge

Honesty, when it applies to ourselves with genuine compassion rather than punishing precision, is not the end of hope; it is the moment hope becomes something you can actually build on. That sentence is the entire architecture of the Acknowledge stage. And it is worth holding before we go any further, because what this chapter asks of you will feel, at first, like it is moving in the wrong direction.

Every instinct in a parent who loves their child as much as you do will resist the full weight of what Acknowledge requires. The instinct says, "I have already looked at this." I have already named it, traced it, grieved it, and tallied its costs. Surely what's needed now is forward motion: the tools, the practices, the new behaviours that will close the distance. Why are we still looking backward?

Here is the answer, and it matters: Because there is a difference between having seen the cost and having genuinely owned it. Between intellectual recognition and the felt, embodied, irrevocable internal decision that what you've seen on that map is going to change not because you've been told to change it, not because you've read a compelling argument for why it matters, but because you have sat with the full honest weight of it long enough that turning back is no longer a live option. That quality of commitment, the kind that doesn't dissolve the first time the old pattern fires, and the anxiety is loud, and the new behaviour feels impossibly hard, is not produced by information. It is produced by genuine ownership. And genuine ownership is what the Acknowledge stage creates.

8.1 The Difference Between Seeing and Owning

Here is a distinction between parents who make lasting change and those who make temporary change. Seeing the pattern means you can describe it accurately. You can tell someone your 10 most frequent Closed Hand behaviours. You can name the fears beneath them. You can articulate the grief layer underneath the fear. You can draw the line from your childhood to your current parenting with reasonable clarity and without too much defensiveness.

Seeing is necessary. It is not sufficient. Owning the pattern means something different. It means sitting with the specific cost of those specific behaviours on a specific person you love, not as an abstraction, not as a general acknowledgement that fear-driven parenting has a negative impact, but as the full, felt, named reality of what has been happening between you and your child across the weeks and months and years that the pattern has been operating.

Owning feels different from seeing. It arrives with emotion rather than with clarity alone. It involves a moment, sometimes quiet, sometimes not, where the cost stops being a concept and becomes a person. Your person. The face you have been loving from behind the walls you didn't know you were building.

That moment is not comfortable. It is not supposed to be. But it is the moment from which every genuinely lasting change in this framework becomes possible, because it is the moment at which you stop managing a problem and start responding to a person. That shift is everything.

8.2 Writing the Cost Inventory in Full

You were introduced to the Cost Inventory in Chapter 4. You may have completed a version. If you did, this is not a repetition; it is a deepening.

Because the cost inventory you write is written from inside the Acknowledge stage, with the full map of the Witness stage behind you. You know more now than you knew in Chapter 4. You have more specific material. You have the grief layer identified. You have the Three-Hand classification applied to your actual behaviours. You have sometimes already run the Three-Second Check in a live interaction and seen something true about the gap between the hand you reached for and the hand you chose.

Write the Cost Inventory again. In full. With that specificity.

Here is the structure, carried forward from Chapter 4 with one important addition:

Dimension 1 — The Cost to Your Child

Write specifically. Use your child's name. Name the behaviours from your Fear Audit and connect each one to its specific impact on your child, on their developing confidence, their sense of their own capability, the messages they have been receiving about whether they are trusted, whether they are competent, whether the relationship with you is a safe place to bring their real self.

Do not write: *I think it has probably affected his confidence.* Write: *Every time I stepped in before he had the chance to handle something himself, I sent him a message he didn't ask to receive. That message, that I didn't believe he could manage without me, is one he has been living inside. I can see it in the way he hesitates before making decisions. I can see it in the way he checks my face before he commits to an answer. I can see it in the way he has stopped bringing me his* actual problems *because he has learned that bringing me a problem means inviting my management of it, not my presence within it.* That level of specificity. That quality of honest, named, felt acknowledgement.

Dimension 2 — The Cost to the Relationship

Write the conversations that didn't happen. The trust that eroded in specific interactions you can name. The version of your child you don't fully know because the relational conditions for genuine openness were never consistently built. Name the moments you can identify where a withdrawal was made, where your child brought something real and left with less than they came with, because the response they received was management rather than presence.

Write also what you don't know, because the cost to the relationship includes the things your child chose not to tell you, and that unknown territory is part of the honest picture.

Dimension 3 — The Cost to Yourself

This dimension receives the least honest attention because the parent who has been focused on their child's needs for years has often lost the habit of acknowledging their own. Write it anyway. Write the version of yourself that has been subsumed by the role. Write the toll of sustained anxiety on your body, your sleep, and your capacity for other relationships. Write the impact on your partnership, if you have one, on the quality of presence available to your partner when anxiety has already consumed most of your emotional resources.

This is not self-pity. This is the complete picture. And the complete picture is what genuine ownership requires.

Dimension 4 — The Forward-Facing Reframe (The New Addition)

This is where the Acknowledge stage departs from the Cost Inventory you wrote in Chapter 4. In that version, the forward-facing reframe was a sentence completion: *"Because I can see this cost clearly, I am now choosing to ____."*

In this version, the reframe becomes a declaration. Not a sentence completion, but a statement, written in your own words, that captures the specific and irrevocable internal decision that this stage produces.

It might sound like this: *"I have looked at what my fear has cost my child, my relationship, and myself, and I am not looking away from it. I am not minimising it, and I am not letting it become a source of shame. I am letting it be what it is: the honest foundation from which I am choosing to build something different. Not because I have to. Because I have seen what staying the same costs, and I am no longer willing to pay that price."*

Write yours. In your own words. From your own felt experience of what you've just written in the three dimensions above. Let it be as long or as short as it needs to be. Let it be private. Let it be real. That declaration is the Acknowledge stage. That is what ownership sounds like.

8.3 The Guilt-Shame Distinction — One More Time

The Acknowledge stage is the place in the framework where the guilt-shame distinction matters most — because the fuller and more honest the Cost Inventory, the louder the shame voice becomes.

You already know this distinction. Guilt says, *"I did something that needs to change."* Shame says, *"I am something that cannot change."* Guilt points forward. Shame collapses inward.

But knowing the distinction intellectually and maintaining it experientially, in the middle of writing a Cost Inventory that names specific costs to a specific child you love with your entire self, are two different things. And the shame voice, when it arrives at this stage, tends to be persuasive. It arrives dressed as honesty. It says, *"You're not minimising anything." You're seeing it clearly. And what you're seeing is that you've failed this child in ways that matter.*

That voice is not honest. It is shame using the language of honesty to prevent you from doing the very thing that would actually help: moving forward.

Here is the response this book offers you for that moment. Not a reframe that bypasses the pain; the pain is real, and it belongs here. But a statement that holds the pain and the possibility simultaneously:

I understand where this pattern came from. I have named the grief beneath it. I have looked honestly at what it has cost. I am not my pattern; **I am the parent who is choosing, with full knowledge of the cost, to build something different. That is not what a failed parent does. That is what a courageous one does.** Keep that statement somewhere accessible. You will need it more than once before this stage is complete.

8.4 The Partner Alignment Assessment

For those navigating this journey within a partnership, whether a marriage, a co-parenting relationship, or any shared parenting arrangement , the Acknowledge stage includes one additional practice that has no equivalent in solo parenting: the Partner Alignment Assessment.

This practice matters for a specific and practical reason: the work you are doing in this framework can be significantly undermined, not through bad intention but through simple misalignment, if the other adult in your child's life is operating from a fundamentally different set of assumptions about what good parenting looks like.

It works in both directions. The partner who is also parenting from the Closed Hand will reinforce the dynamic you are working to change, even as you're changing your part in it. The partner who is parenting from a position of disengagement may interpret your Open Hand practices as weakness or permissiveness and compensate by tightening their own grip. Neither scenario is insurmountable, but both require acknowledgement before they require navigation.

The Partner Alignment Assessment has two parts.

Part 1 — The Honest Appraisal

Write, privately and without showing your partner, an honest assessment of where their parenting currently sits in relation to the Three-Hand model. Not a verdict, but an observation. Which hand do they most frequently reach for? What do you notice about the fears or patterns that might drive their approach? Where do you see alignment with the work you're doing — and where do you see potential friction?

This is not an exercise in building a case against your partner. It is preparation for a conversation — and the parent who goes into that conversation with clarity about what they're navigating will handle it significantly more skilfully than the one who goes in reactive.

Part 2 — The Partner Alignment Conversation

This is one of the most delicate practical challenges in the entire framework, and it deserves to be treated as such. Introducing the concepts of this book to a partner who has not read it, who may feel implicitly criticised by the suggestion that something needs to change, and who may have their own deeply held views about what good parenting looks like is a task that requires a specific approach. The approach has three principles:

Lead with shared love, not shared diagnoses. The opening of this conversation is not: *I've been reading this book, and I've realised that we've both been parenting from* fear, *and it's been damaging our relationship with our child.* That is accurate. It is also almost guaranteed to produce defensiveness. The opening is: *I've been doing some honest thinking about our relationship with [child's name], and I want to share something with you, not because I think you've done anything wrong, but because I think there might be something here for both of us.*

Introduce the language, not the diagnosis. Share the Three-Hand model as a framework rather than as an assessment of your partner's parenting. Ask: *Which hand do you think you reach for most often? Which hand do you think I reach for?* Make it a shared inquiry rather than a reported finding.

Invite, don't recruit. The goal of this conversation is not to get your partner to commit to the entire WALLS Framework in a single discussion. The goal is to establish a shared language, a set of terms and concepts that both of you can use to talk about your parenting in a way that is curious rather than defensive. From that shared language, alignment grows organically over time.

If your partner is resistant, sceptical, or simply not ready for this conversation, that is not a reason to stop. It is a reason to continue your own work, understanding that unilateral change, practised consistently, creates the relational conditions that make partner alignment more possible. You do not need your partner's participation to begin. Their participation, when it arrives, will deepen and multiply the impact of what you're already building.

8.5 From Passive Recognition to Active Ownership

There is a moment in the Acknowledge stage, different for every parent, impossible to predict in advance, and entirely recognisable when it arrives, where the work shifts from something you are doing to something you have decided. It is when the Cost Inventory ceases to be a writing exercise and becomes a commitment. Where the forward-facing declaration stops being words on a page and becomes a statement of intent, you can feel that it is already true. Where the guilt converts cleanly, quietly, and permanently into agency.

This is the moment that research on sustained behaviour change identifies as the most reliable predictor of whether a transformation will last. Not the quality of the insight. Not the sophistication of the tools. The presence or absence of this moment, the irrevocable internal decision, is what separates the parent who makes a lasting change from the parent who makes a temporary adjustment. You cannot manufacture this moment. But you can create the conditions for it, by writing the Cost Inventory with genuine specificity rather than comfortable generality, by naming the costs to a named person rather than to an abstract concept, and by allowing the weight of honest ownership to land fully before moving to the reframe.

When the moment arrives, and if you do this work honestly, you will know it. Not because the pain disappears. But because something underneath the pain solidifies into the particular quality of resolve that does not require ongoing motivation to sustain itself. That resolve is the Acknowledge stage, complete.

And from it, the Loosen stage becomes not just possible but necessary, because the parent who has genuinely owned the cost of the pattern can no longer pretend, even to themselves, that staying in it is a neutral choice.

The Acknowledge Stage at a Glance

Practice	What It Requires	What It Produces
The Full Cost Inventory	Four dimensions written with genuine specificity—child, relationship, self, and the forward-facing declaration	The complete, felt, owned picture of what the pattern has cost and the irrevocable decision to change it
Guilt-Shame Navigation	Recognising the shame voice when it arrives and returning, deliberately, to the guilt that fuels rather than paralyses	The emotional resilience to complete the inventory honestly without collapsing into self-condemnation
Partner Alignment Assessment	An honest private appraisal of partner alignment, followed by the Partner Alignment Conversation using the three-principle approach	A shared language and, over time, a shared direction—or the clarity to proceed powerfully alone

Table 8: Showing the Acknowledge Stage at a Glance

Key Takeaway 8

Acknowledgement, done with compassion and without minimising, is the most liberating act available at this stage. The parent who fully owns the cost of their pattern on their child, their relationship, and themselves, discovers that honesty is not the end of hope. It is the moment hope becomes actionable.

You have seen it clearly. You have owned it completely. The map is behind you, and the first doorway is open. What lies ahead, in Chapter 9 and the Loosen stage, is the most practically demanding work of the entire framework. Not the most emotionally difficult. You have just done that. But the most practically demanding: when the understanding stops and the doing begins. When the new behaviour has to happen in real time, with a real person, in the middle of a real interaction, and the anxiety rises, and the old pattern reaches for the wheel, and you have three seconds to choose differently. You are ready for that. The work of Acknowledgement has made sure of it.

Chapter 9 is the Loosen stage, and it is where the transformation stops being something you understand and becomes something you are actually doing. The Deliberate Step Back. The Evidence File. The daily log of hand-reached *versus* hand-chosen. *This is the chapter where theory becomes practice, where insight becomes action, and where the first real, irrefutable,* experienced *evidence* accumulates *that your child is more capable than your fear has ever* allowed *you to believe. That evidence, once it* builds, *changes something. It always does.*

Chapter Nine

Release The Grip

L — Loosen

Understanding a pattern is not the same as changing it, and the distance between those two things is exactly the width of the Loosen stage. Every parent who arrives at this chapter has done significant work. You have named the pattern, traced its origins, honoured the grief beneath it, reckoned honestly with its cost, and built the map and the compass that the stages ahead require. You have probably developed a clearer understanding of your own parenting in the last eight chapters than you have had at any previous point in your parenting life.

The pattern fires. The anxiety rises. The hand reaches for the phone before the thought has fully formed. The intervention happens before the deliberate choice has had a chance to arrive. This is not a failure of understanding. It is the predictable, entirely normal behaviour of a deeply conditioned neural pathway doing exactly what deeply conditioned neural pathways do: operating faster than conscious thought, in the direction of least resistance, toward the response that has been practised ten thousand times. Understanding does not interrupt that pathway. Practice does.

The Loosen stage is where the practice begins. Not in principle. Not in intention. In the kitchen, in the car, in the middle of a conversation, in the specific charged moment when the old response is the path of least resistance and you have three seconds to choose something different. This is the most practically demanding stage of the entire framework. It is also the stage where the transformation stops being something you're reading about and becomes something you are actually living. Welcome to the work.

9.1 What Loosening Actually Requires

The word loosen suggests something gentle. A gradual relaxation. A slow, comfortable release. That is not what this stage feels like from the inside. From the inside, loosening feels like standing at the edge of something and being asked to step back rather than forward — when every instinct, every conditioned response, every piece of anxious reasoning your nervous system can produce is pointing in the opposite direction. It feels like watching a situation unfold that you could intervene in, and choosing not to, while the catastrophising loop runs its full and vivid programme of everything that might go wrong.

It is uncomfortable. It is supposed to be uncomfortable. And the parent who has been told in advance that the discomfort of not intervening is not evidence of danger, but evidence of growth, is far less likely to misread what they're feeling and retreat to the Closed Hand. So let's say it clearly here, before the practices begin:

The anxiety you feel when you choose not to intervene is not a signal that something is wrong. It is the feeling of a neural pathway being interrupted. It is what change feels like in the nervous system of a person who has been operating from fear for a long time. It is survivable. And every time you survive it, every time you feel it fully and choose the Open Hand anyway, the pathway of deliberate choice grows marginally stronger, and the old pathway grows marginally weaker. That is the biology of what is happening when you practice the Loosen stage. Not a metaphor. The actual, measurable neurological process of rewiring.

9.2 The Three-Hand Method as Your Daily Operating System

In Chapter 6, the Three-Hand Method was introduced as the compass, the real-time diagnostic that bridges the knowing-doing gap in the charged moment. In the Loosen stage, it becomes something more than a tool you use occasionally when you remember to. It becomes your daily operating system.

Every significant parenting interaction gets the Three-Second Check. Not most of them. Not the ones you have time to prepare for. Everyone — because the interactions that most need deliberate choice are precisely the ones that happen fastest, with the least warning, in the moments when you are most tired, most triggered, and least inclined toward reflection.

The Three-Second Check in the Loosen stage has one addition to the version you practised in Chapter 7. After the three questions, Name the Hand, Check the Driver, Choose the Hand, there is a fourth step:

Log it. Not elaborately. Not in a way that requires stopping the interaction to write a paragraph. One line, recorded in the evening, in the daily log: *Interaction: [brief description]. Hand reached for: [Closed/Open/Guiding]. Hand-chosen: [Closed/Open/Guiding]. Gap: [yes/no].* That is the entire entry. Five fields. Thirty seconds.

The log is not a report card. It is not a measure of how well you are doing. It is a data source, and its value lies not in any single entry but in the pattern that emerges across entries. The parent who logs consistently for two weeks will see things in their own pattern that no amount of reflection alone would reveal: the specific times of day when the Closed Hand is most dominant, the specific topics that reliably trigger the high-anxiety responses, the specific interactions where the gap between hand reached and hand chosen is consistently widest.

That information is not available from memory. Memory is selective, and the anxious parent's memory tends to focus on the moments when the pattern was at its worst or most dramatic. The log gives you the complete picture, and that is what precision targeting of your practice requires.

9.3 The Deliberate Step Back

The centrepiece of the Loosen stage is the **Deliberate Step Back**, the practice that more than any other single element of the framework converts the understanding of open-handed parenting into the lived experience of it. Here is how it works.

Choosing the Situation

Return to your Fear Audit from Chapter 7. Look at your list of ten Closed Hand behaviours. Find the one that carries the lowest anxiety charge, the intervention that still belongs in the Closed Hand column but that produces the least intense fear response when you imagine not doing it.

Not the easiest situation in your life. The easiest situation on your specific list. The distinction matters because the Deliberate Step Back is calibrated to start where the neural pathway of deliberate choice can be most successfully established, and then progressively work toward the higher-anxiety situations as the pathway strengthens.

Starting with your highest-anxiety situation is not courage. It is the parenting equivalent of deciding to run a marathon on your first day of training. The anxiety will overwhelm the deliberate choice; the old pattern will reassert itself, and you will have generated evidence that the practice doesn't work, when what actually happened is that it was applied at the wrong intensity for the stage of the training.

Start with the lowest. Build the pathway. The higher-anxiety situations will become accessible from a position of accumulated competence rather than desperate willpower.

Executing the Step Back

In the next instance of the situation you've chosen, the next time it presents itself in real life, with your actual child, apply the following sequence:

1. Notice the impulse. Feel the familiar reach for the Closed Hand. Name it internally: *This is the impulse. I can feel it. It is not an instruction.*

2. Run the Three-Second Check. Name the Hand. Check the Driver. Choose the Open Hand.

3. Do not intervene. Allow the situation to unfold without your managing it. Allow the natural consequence, whatever it is, to land in full, unmodified by your involvement.

4. Stay present without rescuing. This is the part most parents find hardest. Not intervening does not mean disappearing. You can be physically present, emotionally available, and genuinely warm , without stepping in. The Open Hand is not an absent hand. It is a hand that is there, visible, offered ,but not gripping.

5. Observe what actually happens. Not what you feared would happen. What actually happens? Notice it specifically. Note it.

The Three-Question Reflection

After the situation has resolved , that evening, or as soon as you have a quiet moment, write the answers to three questions:

"What did I fear would happen?" Write the catastrophising loop in full. The specific worst-case scenario your anxiety was running while you chose not to intervene. Write it without embarrassment; these fears are not irrational; they are conditioned, and seeing them written is part of the process of developing perspective on them. **"What actually happened?"** Write what actually occurred. Specifically, accurately, and without minimising either the difficulty or the capability of your child showed.

"What does the gap between those two answers tell me?" This is the question that builds the Evidence File, and it is the most important of the three. Because the gap between the feared outcome and the actual outcome is, most times, significantly wider than the anxiety predicted. And that gap, which has been documented and accumulated over time, is the most potent antidote to catastrophizing available. Not because it proves that nothing ever goes wrong. Things go wrong. But because it shows, in your own handwriting, from your own life, with your own child, that your anxiety's predictions have a consistent pattern of overestimating risk and underestimating your child's capability. That pattern, once visible, is very difficult to unsee.

9.4 Building the Evidence File

The **Evidence File** is one of the most quietly powerful tools in the entire framework, and it is almost always underestimated by parents who encounter it for the first time, because it sounds too simple to be as effective as it is. The premise is that the catastrophizing loop driving the Closed Hand is an argument. It argues, loudly, persistently, and with considerable emotional force, that your child cannot handle difficulty without your intervention. That they are not resilient enough, competent enough, or resourced enough to navigate the challenges of their own lives without your management.

The evidence file is the counter-argument. Built from the specific, real, documented instances in which your child handled a difficult situation without parental intervention and showed capability, resilience, or growth. Not in a general sense that your child is capable. Specific entries. Dated. Named. Written in one or two sentences.

15th March: She had the difficult conversation with her teacher herself, without me contacting the school. It went better than I expected, and she seemed genuinely proud of how she handled it.

22nd March: He missed the bus and sorted out an alternative route home without calling me. He arrived safely, slightly later, and found the whole thing funny rather than catastrophic.

3rd April: She didn't get the part in the school production. She was disappointed for a day, and then she was fine. I didn't intervene. She didn't need me to.

Each entry is small. Together, they build something that the anxiety cannot easily dismiss, because it is not theoretical, not aspirational, not borrowed from someone else's child. They are yours. They are real. And they are growing more numerous and more specific with every week that the Loosen stage continues.

The Evidence File does not eliminate the catastrophising loop. What it does is give you something to hold against it when it fires, a body of personal, irrefutable evidence that your anxiety's threat assessment has been consistently, demonstrably, and sometimes dramatically overestimating the danger and underestimating the child.

Add to it every time you complete a Deliberate Step Back. Add to it whenever you notice your child showing capability in any context, not just the ones where you deliberately stepped back. Let it grow. Return to it on the days when the anxiety is loudest and the old pattern feels most compelling. The Evidence File is the antidote that gets stronger every time you use it.

9.5 When the Old Pattern Fires Anyway

It will. Let's be clear about that before it happens. There will be moments in the Loosen stage when the Three-Second Check doesn't happen fast enough, when the anxiety fires at a volume that overwhelms the deliberate choice, when you look up and realise the Closed Hand has already landed and the intervention has already happened before you decided differently. This is not a failure. This is the pattern behaving exactly as deeply conditioned patterns behave, with speed and force and the full weight of ten thousand previous repetitions behind them. The question is not whether this will happen. It will. The question is what you do when it does.

Here is the answer the Loosen stage provides: you treat it as data, not as defeat.

One Closed Hand interaction does not undo the neural pathway of deliberate choice you have been building. It does not reset the Evidence File. It does not prove that change is not happening. It provides one data point, specifically, information about the conditions under which the old pattern is currently strongest, and that information is useful.

After an old-pattern interaction, write three things in your log: *1. What were the conditions? (Time of day, level of stress, specific trigger, quality of sleep, presence of other pressures) 2. What did the interaction cost? (What was the relational impact, however small?) 3. What would I do differently if this situation presented itself again tomorrow?*

That third question is the most important. Because the parent who asks it, who treats the relapse as a design problem rather than a character verdict, is the parent who learns from the pattern faster than the parent who treats it as evidence of fundamental inadequacy.

The Loosen stage is not a performance. It is a practice. Practices have imperfect sessions. What matters is not the perfection of any single session but the consistency of returning to the practice — with the same compassion you have been learning to extend to your child, extended now to yourself.

9.6 The Anxiety Tolerance Reflection

There is one more practice in the Loosen stage that deserves its own section — not because it is complex, but because it addresses something that the Deliberate Step Back and the Evidence File together do not fully cover.

The Deliberate Step Back works with specific, named situations. The Evidence File works with specific, documented outcomes. But there is a dimension of the Loosen stage that operates between those two specific practices in the general, ambient, low-level anxiety that persists between interventions, which colours the quality of the parent's presence even when no specific situation presents itself.

The **Anxiety Tolerance Reflection** is a brief, daily written practice, three to five minutes maximum, designed to build the parent's capacity to be with anxiety rather than act on it. Not to eliminate the anxiety. Not to medicate it or argue it away. Build the tolerance for sitting with it long enough that it no longer automatically triggers the Closed Hand response.

Each evening, after completing the daily log, write the answers to two questions:

"What anxiety did I carry today that I did not act on?" This question reframes not-acting as an achievement, which it is, particularly in the early stages of the Loosen practice. The parent who carried anxiety and did not act on it has done something that deserves to be named.

"What did I discover about my capacity to tolerate discomfort today?" This is the capacity-building question. Not *was the anxiety comfortable* — it wasn't. But *was it survivable?* And the answer, almost always, is yes. Building a conscious, documented record of that survivability gradually expands the parent's window of tolerance for the discomfort that open-handed parenting requires.

The Loosen Stage at a Glance

Practice	What It Requires	What It Produces
Three-Hand Method as a Daily Operating System	Every significant interaction gets the Three-Second Check, logged nightly in five fields	A precise, accumulating map of the pattern's strongest conditions and the deliberate choice's growing competence
The Deliberate Step Back	Lowest-anxiety Closed Hand behaviour identified, intervention withheld, three-question reflection completed	The first real, lived, personally irrefutable experience that not intervening produces survivable outcomes and capable children
The Evidence File	One to two sentence entries added after every Deliberate Step Back and every observed instance of child capability	A growing body of personal evidence that dismantles the catastrophising loop more effectively than any argument
The Anxiety Tolerance Reflection	Two questions answered nightly in three to five minutes	An expanding window of tolerance for the discomfort of the Open Hand, built through the documented record of survivability

Table 9: Showing Loosen Stage at a Glance

Key Takeaway 9

Loosening is not passive; **it is the most practically demanding stage of the entire framework.** The discomfort of not intervening is not evidence of danger; it is evidence of growth. Every deliberate act of trust, however small, accumulates into a new neural pathway that gradually replaces the fear-driven default with the Open Hand.

You are not doing nothing when you choose not to intervene. You are doing the hardest thing this framework asks of you. You are choosing, in real time, against the full force of a conditioned pattern, and building, one repetition at a time, the neural architecture of a different kind of love. That is not a minor act. It is, in every meaningful sense, the act this entire book has been building toward.

The Loosen stage does not end on a specific date. It ends when the Three-Hand Check has become sufficiently habitual that the deliberate choice is arriving faster than the old response, not always, not perfectly, but consistently enough that the Open Hand is no longer a heroic effort and has begun to feel like a genuinely available option.

When that shift happens ,and you will feel it before you can fully articulate it, you are ready for the Listen stage. Chapter 10 is where the bridge gets built. Not through changed behaviour alone, but through the specific quality of attention that your child has been waiting, perhaps for longer than either of you knows, to receive from you. The Loosen stage cleared the ground. The Listen stage builds on it.

Chapter Ten

Hear What They're Actually Saying

L — Listen

The most common mistake a parent makes when they decide to listen better is believing that listening is about what they do with their ears. It isn't. Listening, genuine relationship-building, bridge-constructing listening, is about what you do with your agenda. Specifically, it is about what you will set down long enough to hear what is actually being said, rather than what you were already prepared to respond to.

The parent who has completed the Loosen stage has done something significant: they have changed what they do. They have withheld interventions that previously felt automatic. They have allowed consequences to land. They have built an Evidence File that is shifting the catastrophising loop's grip on their nervous system. The behaviour has changed, measurably, deliberately, and at considerable personal cost.

But behaviour alone does not rebuild a relationship. Not this kind of relationship. Not the one that has been shaped by years of the Closed Hand, where the child has learned, through accumulated experience, not through a single conversation, that their parent's involvement comes at a price. The price of compliance, of reporting, of the ongoing surrender of privacy and autonomy that the Closed Hand requires.,Changed behaviour creates the conditions for a changed relationship. It does not, by itself, create the relationship.

What creates the relationship is the quality of the conversation between the parent and child after the behaviour has changed. And specifically, it is what the parent does with the silence: the space between question and answer, between offering and receiving, between the conversation that was and the conversation that could be. That space is where the Listen stage lives. And learning to inhabit it without filling it with anxiety is the central work of this chapter.

10.1 Why Listening Has Been So Hard

Let's be honest about something that most parenting content skips entirely. For the parent operating from the Closed Hand, listening has not simply been difficult; it has been actively undermined by the anxiety that has been running the relationship. Because genuine listening requires a quality of presence that anxiety makes almost structurally impossible.

Anxiety is not present. It is future-oriented, constantly scanning ahead for what might go wrong, what might need managing, and what the child's words right now might mean for a situation that hasn't happened yet. The anxious parent who appears to be listening is, many times, actually preparing. Preparing their response. Preparing their reframe. Preparing the gentle redirection toward the outcome they prefer. Preparing the lesson that the child's experience is about to become.

The child on the receiving end of that quality of attention learns something quickly. They learn that talking to their parents is not a conversation; it is a consultation. And consultations have outcomes. Outcomes that are, to some significant measure, predetermined by the parent's anxiety rather than shaped by the child's experience. So the child edits. They offer the version of their experience that is least likely to trigger the parental management response. They protect themselves and their autonomy by giving their parents access to the surface while keeping the depth for themselves, for their friends, their journal, the internal life they are carefully building at a distance from the parent who loves them too hard to hear them clearly.

That editing is not deception. It is self-preservation. And the parent who wants to hear what is actually being said must first create the conditions under which their child believes that honesty with them is safe. Those conditions are built through the Open Question practice, the Repair Conversation, and the Consistency Protocol, and they are built slowly over time through the cumulative quality of every interaction that follows the decision to truly listen.

10.2 The Open Question Practice

The first tool of the Listen stage is the **Open Question practice**, and it is worth beginning with an explicit statement of what makes a question open, because the difference between an open question and a closed one is not grammatical. It is intentional.

A closed question is one that has a preferred answer. The parent who asks *"Did you have a good day?"* is not genuinely inquiring; they are hoping for a yes, and both parties know it. The parent who asks, *"Are you sure that's a good idea?"* is not asking at all; they are delivering a verdict in interrogative clothing. The parent who asks, *"Have you thought about what happens if this doesn't work out?"* is not exploring with their child; they are using the question as a vehicle for anxiety management that genuine listening would require them to set down.

Closed questions close doors. They signal to the child receiving them that the conversation is not a safe space for a genuine response, because a genuine response is not actually what's being sought.

An open question is genuinely curious. It has no preferred answer. It is asked in the specific, present-tense interest of hearing what this person actually thinks, feels, wants, or experiences, not as data for parental assessment, not as an opportunity for redirection, but as an intrinsically valuable piece of knowledge about a person the parent loves and is still, after all these years, learning. Here are the five Open Question structures that consistently invite a genuine response from a teenager or young adult without triggering defensiveness or the sense of being managed·

Structure 1 — The Pure Curiosity Question

"What was the best part of today?" *"What are you most looking forward to this week?"* *"What's been on your mind lately?"* These questions have no subtext. They are not checking. They are not assessing. They are simply curious — and they signal, to the child receiving them, that the parent's interest is genuine rather than strategic.

Structure 2 — The Experience Question

"What was that like for you?" "How did that feel in the moment?" "What did you make of it afterwards?" These questions prioritise the child's subjective experience over the objective facts of a situation. They communicate that the parent is interested not in what happened, but in what it meant to the person it happened . This distinction between a parent interested in facts and a parent interested in experience is one that teenagers, in particular, are exquisitely sensitive to.

Structure 3 — The Perspective Question

"What do you think you'll do?" "What's your instinct on this?" "If you had to decide today, what would you decide?" These questions communicate trust. They signal that the parent believes the child has a perspective worth hearing — and that they are interested in that perspective for its own sake, not as a prelude to correction.

Structure 4 — The Reflection Question

"Looking back, what would you do differently?" "What did you learn from how that went?" "What do you know now that you didn't know before?" These questions invite self-reflection without imposing the parent's assessment of what the reflection should conclude. They position the child as the authority on their own experience, which is both accurate and, in this relationship, profoundly connecting.

Structure 5 — The Future Question

"What would make that easier next time?" "What do you need to feel more ready for that?" "What would help?" These questions are forward-facing without being prescriptive. They offer the parents' investment in the child's future without substituting the parents' solutions for the child's own. The child who is asked, *"What would help?"* rather than told *"Here's what you should do"* receives a message that is, in the Closed Hand history, genuinely radical: *I believe you can work out what you need. I am here if you want me involved, but this is yours.*

10.3 The Discipline of Listening Without Preparing

Learning the five structures is the easier part of the Open Question practice. The harder part — the part that requires the same deliberate, practised, logged discipline that the Loosen stage brought to the Deliberate Step Back is developing the capacity to listen to the answer without simultaneously preparing a response. This is where most parents underestimate the work involved. They introduce an open question; they receive a genuine answer, and then — before the child has finished speaking, sometimes before they've finished their first sentence — the parent's mind is already composing. Composing the reflection. Composing the gentle challenge. Composing the follow-up that steers the conversation toward the insight they believe the child needs to arrive at.

The child feels this. Not always consciously. But they feel the quality of presence shift from receiving to preparing, and when that shift happens consistently, they stop offering the genuine answers that the open questions were designed to invite. Here is the practice for developing the discipline of genuine listening: **In the moment of listening, do one thing only: be curious about the next word.** Not the conclusion. Not the implication. Not what the words mean for a situation that hasn't happened yet. The next word. What are they actually saying right now in this sentence?

This is harder than it sounds for a parent whose nervous system has been primed for threat assessment. But it is a practical skill — and like every other skill in this framework, it builds with repetition. After the interaction, add one line to your daily log:

*"I listened without preparing: [yes/partially/no]. The moment I started preparing was
_____."* The log does not judge the answer. It notices it. And the pattern that emerges, the specific triggers that reliably cause the shift from receiving to preparing, gives you the precise targets for your continued practice.

10.4 The Repair Conversation

The second major practice of the Listen stage is the **Repair** Conversation, and it is, without question, the most emotionally significant single act this framework asks of you. Not because it is complicated. The framework for it is simple. But because it requires something that the fear-driven parenting years have made genuinely difficult: the willingness to be vulnerable in your child's presence without knowing in advance how they will respond. Here is what the Repair Conversation does and does not involve. **It does not involve:** a comprehensive accounting of everything that went wrong. A detailed apology for specific incidents. An explanation of the psychological origins of your pattern. A request for your child's forgiveness. An expectation of any response. **It** involves three things, and three things only. The Three Elements of the Repair Conversation.

1. "I see what has been happening between us." This is the acknowledgement stated simply, without elaboration, without the defensive qualifications that the fear of vulnerability produces. Not, *I've been* overprotective *sometimes.* Not that *I know, I can be a lot to deal with.* Simply: I see what has been happening. The clarity of that statement, its honesty, its absence of minimisation, communicates something to the child that no amount of changed behaviour can communicate on its own: that the parent is genuinely, honestly aware.

2. "I am working on changing my part in it." This is the ownership, and it is deliberately phrased in the present continuous tense. Not *I have changed.* Not *I am going* to do *better. I am working on* it right now, actively, with specific practices that are already underway. This phrasing is important because a child who has heard promises of change before will not trust a declaration of completion. But they can usually hear, and sometimes believe, a statement of ongoing effort, particularly when the changed behaviour of the Loosen stage has already provided some evidence that the words are not empty.

3. "I am not asking you to respond; I am showing you something different." This is the release I and it is the element that most parents find hardest to deliver without qualification. Because the parent who has opened themselves up to this level of vulnerability wants something in return. They want acknowledgement. They want reciprocity. They want the moment to be received the way they intended it: as a turning point, a threshold, a new beginning.

But asking for that response, even implicitly, through the quality of expectant attention, converts the Repair Conversation from a gift into a transaction. And the child who has been managed for years will experience a transaction differently than they will experience a gift. The transaction asks them for something. The gift simply offers.

Releasing the outcome, genuinely, not performatively, is the most important element of the Repair Conversation. And it is only possible if the parent has fully completed the Acknowledge stage and arrived at the genuine, felt conviction that their work is for the relationship's benefit, not for the validation that the relationship's improvement will provide them. When to Have the Repair Conversation. Not immediately. The Repair Conversation belongs in the Listen stage, not the Loosen stage, because it requires that the foundation of changed behaviour be laid first.

The child who receives the Repair Conversation before any behavioural change has occurred will receive it as words. The child who receives it after several weeks of noticing that something is genuinely different, that the follow-up texts have reduced, that the consequences have been allowed to land, that the questions being asked have a different quality, will receive it as a confirmation of what they have already observed.

Timing matters. When you feel the behavioural changes of the Loosen stage are sufficiently established, when your Evidence File has enough entries that the Open Hand is feeling like a genuine alternative rather than a heroic effort, you are ready for the Repair Conversation.

Choose a moment that is private, unhurried, and low-stakes in its setting. Not in the middle of a conflict. Not as a prelude to a tough conversation. Simply, a moment. A quiet one. And then say the three things. Clearly, simply, and without waiting to see if they land the way you hoped. Then release it.

10.5 The Consistency Protocol

The third practice of the Listen stage is the **Consistency Protocol,** the daily, weekly, and monthly practice structure that converts the insights and tools of this chapter from a reading experience into a living habit. Because here is the truth about everything this chapter has offered: it will not change the relationship if it is applied occasionally, when the parent remembers, on the days when conditions are favourable. It will change the relationship if it is applied consistently, on the hard days, on the days when the child is not receptive, on the days when the old pattern fires and the Open Question lands with a closed door.

Consistency in this context is not stubbornness. It is the signal that the change is real. And the child who has learned not to trust that change is real will not respond to one pleasant conversation or two weeks of change. They will respond to the accumulated, unmistakable evidence of a parent who keeps showing up differently, not because the child is reciprocating, but because the parent has genuinely changed. Here is the Consistency Protocol:

Daily — the five-minute check-in. One genuine, Open Question-structured interaction per day. Not a long conversation. Not an interrogation. One question asked with genuine curiosity, followed by genuine listening, followed by a logged note. Five minutes. Every day. The accumulation of these interactions is what the child notices, not any single one, but the pattern of them.

Weekly — the twenty-minute review. Once per week, review the daily log. Identify the two moments of most successful Open Hand listening and the two moments of most significant Closed Hand pull. Write one sentence about what each of the difficult moments had in common. This is the pattern-recognition work that the daily log makes possible: the level above the individual entry, where the larger shape of your progress and your remaining work becomes visible.

Monthly — the sixty-minute WALLS assessment. Once per month, return to the full WALLS Framework. Assess, honestly and with the map fully in view, where you are in each stage. Not where you hoped to be, but where you are. The monthly assessment prevents the common pattern of progress followed by invisible regression because the parent who checks their position on the map regularly will notice drift before it becomes distance.

The Listen Stage at a Glance

Practice	Requires	Produces
The Open Question Practice	Five specific question structures used daily, with genuine listening—without preparing, redirecting, or filling silence.	Creates conditions where a self-protective child begins to offer a genuine response.
The Repair Conversation	Three elements only, delivered vulnerably and without outcome expectation, after sufficient behavioral evidence.	Acknowledges what has been happening—and that the parent is responsible for change.
The Consistency Protocol	Daily 5-minute check-in, weekly 20-minute review, and monthly 60-minute WALLS assessment.	Provides sustained evidence of change that a child will eventually begin to believe.

Table 10: Showing the Listen at a glance stage

Key Takeaway 10

Genuine listening, agenda-free, outcome-independent, and sustained over time, is the single most powerful bridge-building act available to any **parent.** The child who experiences a parent who asks without managing and listens without correcting will, almost always and eventually, move toward them. The relationship does not rebuild in one conversation. It rebuilds in the accumulated quality of every conversation that follows this one.

You are not waiting for a single breakthrough moment. You are building something: one question, one silence held, one outcome released at a time. And what you are building is more durable than anything a breakthrough moment could produce, because it is built not from intensity but from consistency. That is what your child has been waiting for. Not a different parent. The same parent, finally present enough to hear them.

The Soars stage, *the final doorway of the WALLS Framework, is where the transformation completes itself. Not by arriving at a destination and stopping, but by becoming the parent whose life is full enough, whose identity is whole enough, and whose love is open-handed enough that the relationship with their child becomes the richest thread in a rich fabric rather than the only thread in an empty one.*

Chapter 11 is where you find out who you are when you are not managing your child's life. And what most parents discover, when they look, is that the answer is more interesting than the fear ever allowed them to believe.

Chapter Eleven

Step Into The Life You Were Building Toward

S — Soar

There is a question that has been sitting underneath every other question in this book, quieter than the fear, less urgent than the grief, easier to defer than the cost inventory, and it is the question that the Soar stage finally asks out loud: **Who are you when you are not managing your child's life?** Not who you were before the children arrived. Not who you plan to become once the relationship is fully repaired, the anxiety is fully resolved, and the conditions are finally right. Who are you now, in this season, with this life, with everything you have learned across the chapters behind you, when the parenting role is not consuming every available dimension of your identity?

Most parents in your position have not answered this question recently. Some have not answered it in years. The intensive parenting season — and fear-driven parenting is an intensive season , has a way of quietly narrowing the self until the role and the person become almost indistinguishable. Until the parent who is asked what they enjoy, what they want, what matters to them outside the family, reaches for an answer and discovers that the shelf where that answer used to sit has been empty for longer than they realised.

The Soar stage is where you restock that shelf. Not as a reward for completing the earlier stages. Not as a self-care addendum to the actual work of the framework. As the final and most strategically important stage of a transformation that has been building from the very first page of this book, toward a single destination: the parent whose child chooses to call. Because here is what the research, and the experience of every parent who has walked this path before you, confirms without exception: the parent whose life is full enough that they are genuinely interesting, genuinely present, and genuinely available, rather than consumed, depleted, and oriented entirely around the child's life, is the parent their child finds most worth returning to. The Soar stage is not a detour from the relationship you are building. It is the most direct route to it.

11.1 The Identity Question

Let's sit with the identity question for a moment before we move to the practices, because it deserves more than a passing acknowledgement. The loss of self within the parenting role is one of the most common and least discussed costs of intensive parenting. It happens gradually, invisibly, and almost always with the full cooperation of the parent it is happening to, because at each stage of the narrowing, the sacrifice feels like love. The hobby is set aside because there simply isn't time. The ambition was quietly shelved because the children needed consistency. The friendship allowed to fade because the energy required to maintain it has been redirected to the family. The question of personal passion deferred month after month until it stops being deferred and simply becomes gone.

None of these sacrifices were wrong. Many of them were genuinely necessary in the season in which they were made. But the parent who arrives at the Soar stage carrying all of them, carrying the accumulated weight of a self that has been progressively subordinated to a role, is carrying something that affects the relationship in ways they may not fully recognize.

Because a parent without a self of their own places, inevitably, unconsciously, and with no malicious intent, an excessive weight of meaning on the parent-child relationship. That relationship becomes not just one important relationship among several, but the primary, sometimes the only, source of the parent's sense of purpose, connection, and identity. And that weight, that quality of being someone's entire world — is precisely what drives a child toward the door.

Not because they don't love you. Because they cannot breathe inside the responsibility of being your entire world. Because the most loving thing they can do for both of you is to create enough distance that you are forced, eventually, to find your own.

The Soar stage makes that finding deliberate rather than forced. It invites you to reclaim your own life, not because the relationship demands it but because you deserve it, and because the version of you that exists on the other side of that reclamation is, without exception, the parent your child is most capable of genuinely choosing.

11.2 The Identity Reclamation Practice

The first tool of the Soar stage is the **Identity Reclamation Practice**, a four-week, structured investment in one area of personal passion, interest, or ambition that belongs entirely to you, outside the parenting role. Not a vague commitment to self-care. Not a resolution to be kinder to yourself. A specific, named, scheduled, weekly investment in something that matters to you as a person, not as a parent, not as a partner, not as an employee or a neighbour or any of the other roles that constitute the social self, but as the individual who existed before any of those roles were assumed and who will exist after each of them has strengthened. Here is the four-week structure:

Week 1 — The Rediscovery

Write, without filtering or editing, the answers to these three questions:

"Before the intensive parenting years, what did I do that made me feel most like myself?"

"If time, money, and other people's expectations were not factors, what would I spend more of my life doing?"

"What have I told myself I would do 'when things settle down' for long enough that I've stopped believing things will settle down?"

Do not assess the answers for practicality. Do not immediately move to the question of how. Write what is true. The purpose of Week 1 is not to produce a plan; it is to surface the answer to the identity question that has been waiting, sometimes for years, for permission to be honestly stated. From the answers, choose one thing. One interest, passion, or ambition. It does not need to be grand. It does not need to be impressive. It needs to be genuinely yours, something that, when you write it down, produces a flicker of something that is not anxiety and not obligation, and not the feeling of doing what you should. Something that feels, however faintly, like *yes*.

Week 2 — The First Hour

This week, invest one hour in the thing you named in Week 1. One hour. Scheduled. Protected. Treated with the same seriousness as an appointment you would not cancel without a significant reason. This will feel disproportionately difficult for many parents. The guilt will arrive with the familiar voice that says this hour should be spent on something more useful, more productive, more oriented toward the people who need you. That voice is the residue of the intensive parenting years operating in a new context. It is not an instruction. It is a habit.

Do it anyway. And afterwards, write one sentence in your log: *"I spent an hour on____, and it felt____."*

The feeling named in that sentence, whatever it is, including if it is rusty or uncomfortable or unfamiliar — is information. It is the beginning of knowing what your own life feels like from the inside, after years of experiencing it primarily from the outside of someone else's.

Week 3: The Expansion

This week, increase the investment. Not dramatically, not from one hour to twenty. From one hour to two, or from one session to two sessions. The expansion is not about volume. It is about establishing the practice as a regular feature of your week rather than a one-off experiment. It is also, in Week 3, about telling someone. Not everyone. One person, a friend, a partner, a trusted colleague, that you have started doing this thing. That you are investing in this part of yourself. That it matters to you.

The act of naming it to another person does something that private practice alone cannot do: it makes it real in the social world. It creates a small but genuine accountability. And it begins, slowly, to rebuild the identity that has been narrowed, because you are now, to at least one other person, someone who does this thing. Someone who has this interest. Someone who is more than their parenting role.

Week 4: The Integration

In Week 4, the practice becomes a permanent feature of your life, not a phase, not a project, but an ongoing, non-negotiable investment in the person who is also, and always, the parent. Write a brief, practical commitment: how many times per week, for how long, in what specific context, this investment will continue. Put it in your diary. Treat its protection as a matter of self-respect rather than self-indulgence.

And then, at the end of Week 4, answer the identity question again:

"Who am I when I am not managing my child's life?"

Compare your answer to the one you couldn't fully access at the beginning of this stage. Notice what has shifted — not just in what you've written, but in the quality of presence from which you wrote it.

11.3 Defining Your Flourish Markers

The second practice of the Soar stage is identifying **Flourish Markers** — the specific, emotionally meaningful indicators that will tell you, with personal precision, that the transformation is real. Not generic milestones. Not the ones this book suggests, or those of another parent's journey produced. The ones that matter to you and to this relationship specifically, the precise moments that would tell the version of you who opened this book that the journey was worth every difficult page. Here is how to identify them.

Close your eyes for a moment, or simply stop reading and think, genuinely, without the pressure of having to write anything yet. Think about the relationship you want with your child. Not the relationship you're afraid you'll never have. The one you actually want. The one that, when you allow yourself to imagine it without immediately dismissing it as fantasy, produces something in your chest that is lighter than the anxiety and warmer than the grief. What does it look like? Not in general terms, but in specific ones. Is it the voluntary phone call, the one they make not because they feel they should, but because something happened and you're the person they want to tell? Is it the Sunday dinner chosen freely, the invitation accepted not from obligation but because your home is a place they actually want to be? Is it the real conversation ,the one where they bring something genuine, something difficult, exciting, or uncertain, and you receive it without managing it? Is it the moment they introduce you to someone important in their life, not as a duty but as a pleasure?

Write three to five moments. With as much sensory and emotional specificity as you can bring to them. Not as hopes, — as images. Clear, detailed images of the relationship as it will be when the open-handed love you are building has had the time and the consistency it needs to become the relationship's natural climate.

These are your Flourish Markers. They are the face of the destination, specific enough to orient toward in the difficult moments when the progress feels slow, and the anxiety is loud, and the old pattern is pulling hard. Return to them on those days. Not as a measure of how far you still have to go, but as a reminder of what you are building toward and why the building is worth the cost.

11.4 The Legacy Letter

The final practice of the Soar stage, and of the entire WALLS Framework, is **The Legacy Letter**. This is a private, unsealed letter written to your child. It will not be sent. It is not a communication. It is a commitment, the clearest possible articulation, in your own words and your own handwriting, of the parent you have become, the relationship you are building, and the love you now offer with open hands. Here is what it contains:

Part 1 — What I Have Seen

Write to your child directly about what you have seen across the journey this book has taken you on. Not a comprehensive account of every insight; the letter is not a report. But the essential thing: that you have seen what has been happening between you, that you have understood your part in it with honesty and without minimising, and that what you have seen has changed you in ways that are real and permanent. Write this in your own voice. Not the voice of a parent delivering a lesson. The voice of a person speaking honestly to someone they love.

Part 2 — What I Am Building

Write what you are building toward, not in framework language, but in the relationship's language itself. The specific moments you named in your Flourish Markers. The quality of presence you are learning to offer. The conversations you want to have and the ones you are learning to receive. The version of you that your child deserves to have access to is the parent who is interested in who they are becoming, not just in whether they are safe.

Part 3 — What I Now Know About Love

Write the truth that this book has been building toward since the Introduction. In your own words. From your own hard-won experience of what it has cost to learn it. That the love that lasts is always the love that does not demand to be held. That the open hand holds more than the closed fist ever could. That the relationship you have been fighting for, the one you opened this book hoping to find, was never somewhere else. It was always here, on the other side of the fear that has been speaking louder than your love for years.

Write about that. In whatever words are true for you. As long as it needs to be or as short as it needs to be. And then fold it, put it somewhere safe, and keep it. Not as a document of where you were. As evidence of where you are, and of the love you are now offering, with open hands, to the person who has always deserved it most.

11.5 What Soar Actually Means

The word soar suggests effortlessness. A release into something easier. And there is an element of that, because the parent who has moved through Witness, Acknowledge, Loosen, and Listen arrives at Soar carrying significantly less than they were carrying when they opened Chapter 1. Less fear. Less unacknowledged grief. Less of the pattern's unconscious weight. Less of the exhaustion that comes from parenting two lives simultaneously.

But Soar is not the end of the effort. It is the beginning of a distinct effort, an ongoing, deliberate, joyful effort of maintaining an open hand through the inevitable challenges of real family life. The disagreements that will still arise. The life choices that will still be difficult to watch. The seasons of natural distance that are healthy and no longer catastrophic. The moments when the old pattern stirs, and the Three-Second Check stands between the relationship as it is and the relationship as it was.

Soar requires tending. It is a living state, not a fixed one. And the parent who tends it, who returns to the Consistency Protocol in the difficult seasons, who adds to the Evidence File even when the relationship is going well, who keeps investing in the Identity

Reclamation Practice even after the initial urgency has faded, is the parent who discovers what the fear never allowed them to believe:

The relationship on the other side of open-handed love is not the relationship they repaired. It is something neither parent nor child could have built while the grip was still in place. It is better.

The Soar Stage at a Glance

Practice	What It Requires	What It Produces
The Identity Reclamation Practice	Four weeks of structured, increasing investment in one named personal passion or interest	The beginning of a self that exists independently of the parenting role—and the parent their child finds most genuinely interesting to return to
Flourish Markers	Three to five specific, emotionally precise images of the relationship as it will be when the transformation is real	A face for the destination—specific enough to orient toward in the difficult moments when progress feels slow
The Legacy Letter	Three parts: what I have seen, what I am building, what I now know about love—written privately, kept permanently	The clearest possible evidence, in the parent's own words, that the love they are offering has been genuinely transformed

Table 11: Showing the Soar Stage at a Glance

Key Takeaway 11

Soar is not a destination the reader arrives at once and inhabits forever. It is a living state that requires ongoing tending, and the parent who reaches it discovers something the fear never allowed them to believe: the relationship waiting on the other side of open-handed love is not the relationship they repaired. It is better than anything the grip was trying to protect.

You have walked through all five doorways. You have done the work that most parents never do, not because they love their children less, but because nobody ever gave them the map, the compass, or the permission to see the pattern clearly enough to change it.

You have all three now. And the relationship you have been building toward, one deliberate choice, one open question, one released outcome at a time, is not somewhere in the distance. It is already, in the accumulated quality of every choice you have made since Chapter 1, beginning to take shape.

Part II is complete. The WALLS Framework has been walked in full. Part II gave you the framework. Part III gives you the resilience to live inside it — on the days when it is working and on the days that will come, when it feels like it isn't.

Chapter 12 begins with the hardest of those days. And what you'll discover there may surprise you: those days are not evidence that the framework has failed. They are the most important part of it.

Part III: Flourishing

Part III begins now. But the work of Part III is not less important — it's where the transformation is tested, sustained, and extended into the hardest real-world applications. The chapters ahead address what happens in the real, imperfect, sometimes non-linear terrain of the transformation once it is underway — the seasons when nothing seems to work, the challenge of the co-parenting relationship, the specific applications to adult children and resistant teenagers, and the particular challenge of sustaining open-handed love through the ongoing difficulties of real family life.

Chapter Twelve

When Nothing Seems to Be Working

There will be a day, possibly several, when you do everything this book has asked of you and the relationship feels exactly as distant as it did before you began. You will run the Three-Second Check. You will ask the Open Question. You will hold the silence instead of filling it, release the outcome instead of chasing it, choose the Open Hand instead of the Closed one. You will do all of it with genuine care and genuine effort, and the full weight of everything you have understood across the chapters behind you. **And your child will walk past you without a word.**

Or they will give the minimal response: the monosyllable, the shrug, the glance at the phone that signals the conversation is over before it began. Or they will say something that is not quite hostile but carries enough edge to make the old pattern fire at full volume, and you will feel, standing in your own kitchen with the Open Hand you have worked so hard to build, that none of it is working. The distance is not closing. That the transformation is happening in you and nowhere else. This chapter is for that day. Not to fix it, there is no fix for the specific, grinding difficulty of sustained effort in the absence of visible reward. But to give it a framework that transforms it from evidence of failure into something far more useful and far more honest: evidence that you are inside the most important part of the process.

12.1 What Silence From Your Child Actually Means

The child who has been managed for months or years does not respond to changed parental behaviour the way the parent hopes they will. The parent hopes, understandably, entirely reasonably, that the changed behaviour will be received as the gift it is. That the child will notice the Open Questions and feel the quality of genuine curiosity in them. That they will observe the absence of follow-up texts and experience it as trust. That they will receive the Repair Conversation and feel the honesty. That the relationship will begin, visibly and encouragingly, to warm. Sometimes this happens. Not always.

And for many parents, particularly those whose children are teenagers, or whose relationships have been strained for a significant period, the initial response to changed parental behaviour is not warmth. It is a suspicion. Because here is what the child who has been managed for years has learned: change is temporary. Their parents have tried before. Has been warmer before. Has backed off before. Has promised, explicitly or implicitly, that things would be different, and then, under the pressure of a difficult situation or a spike of anxiety, things have returned to the pattern the child knows as the relationship's true shape. That child is not being cruel when they respond to your Open Hand with a closed door. They are being rational. They are protecting themselves from the particular disappointment of believing that this time is different and then discovering, as they have discovered before, that it isn't. The silence, the monosyllable, the edge in the voice, these are not rejections of who you are becoming. They are the residue of who you have been. And the only response to residue is time. Consistent, patient, unrewarded, Open Hand time , until the evidence accumulates that this change is not temporary. That is what the child is waiting for. Not a better conversation. A longer pattern.

12.2 The Rupture Recovery Tool

Every parent who is working through this framework will experience moments of relapse, moments when the old pattern fires faster than the deliberate choice, when the Closed Hand lands before the Three-Second Check has had a chance to run, when the anxiety speaks before the Open Hand has responded. In those moments, and they will come, in every season of this work, including the seasons when the practice is going well, the parent needs a specific, structured tool for returning to the framework without self-flagellation and without the shame spiral that converts a temporary relapse into evidence of permanent inadequacy. The **Rupture Recovery Tool** is that structure. It is a three-step sequence, designed to be completed within twenty-four hours of an old-pattern interaction.

Step 1: Name It Without Narrative

Write in one sentence what happened. Not an analysis. Not a contextualised account of the pressures that contributed to it. Not a defence. One sentence, naming the behaviour specifically. *"I sent the follow-up text even though I knew she hadn't asked me to check in." "I rewrote his opening paragraph and told him I was just tidying it." "I raised my voice when the conversation didn't go the way I needed it to."* One sentence. The behaviour, named plainly.

The purpose of this step is precision without narrative — because narrative is where shame breeds. The parent who spends forty minutes reconstructing the full context of why the relapse happened is not processing a rupture. They are building a case, either for the defence (justifying the behaviour) or for the prosecution (indicting themselves as unable to change). Neither is useful. The plain named behaviour is.

Step 2: Identify the Condition

Write the answer to this question: *"Under what specific conditions did the old pattern fire?"* Not why you are the way you are , you have already done that work in Chapters 2 and 3. The specific conditions of this specific interaction. The time of day. The level of existing stress. The particular topic. The quality of the exchange that preceded it. The presence or absence of sleep, of support, of the daily practice that would have made the deliberate choice more available.

This step treats the relapse as a design problem rather than a character verdict. The parent who knows that their Closed Hand is most dominant at 9 pm when they haven't slept well, and their child has been uncommunicative all day, has information they can work with. They can adjust the conditions, go to bed earlier, practice the Three-Second Check specifically in that window, build in a brief grounding practice before the evening's interactions begin. The pattern has conditions. Knowing the conditions is the first step toward disrupting them.

Step 3 — The Return Commitment

Write a single commitment for the next twenty-four hours. Not a comprehensive recommitment to the entire framework. One specific and achievable, that returns you to the Open Hand in the relationship's next interaction. *"Tomorrow morning, before I see her, I will run the Three-Second Check on the first interaction of the day." "The next time he's in the room with me, I will ask one Open Question and listen without preparing a response." "I will not send a check-in text today, regardless of how long the silence is."* One commitment. Written. Kept.

The Rupture Recovery Tool does not pretend that the relapse didn't happen. It does not minimise the relational cost of an old-pattern interaction or wave away the difficulty of returning to the practice after a setback. What it does is treat the relapse as data — specific, workable, forward-pointing data, rather than as a verdict.

And the parent who treats their own relapses the way they have been learning to treat their child's mistakes, with honesty, with compassion, and with the clear-eyed commitment to learn from rather than be defined by them, is modelling something that is, in itself, one of the most important things they can model. They are modelling what it looks like to fail and return without shame. And that model, seen by a child who is watching far more closely than they appear to be, is part of the transformation.

12.3 Resistance Versus Awareness

Here is a distinction that will sustain you through the longest and hardest stretches of the Soar stage. Your child's resistance to the change you are making is not the same as your child's unawareness of it.

These two things can look identical from the outside. The child who is actively resisting the parent's changed behaviour looks, in many interactions, exactly like the child who has noticed nothing has changed. The closed door, the monosyllable, the edge in the voice— these are the same whether the child is resisting or simply hasn't yet registered that something is different. But they are not the same from the child's perspective.

The child who is resisting has noticed. They have noticed that the follow-up texts have reduced. They have noticed that the question being asked sounds different from the ones asked before. They noticed that the consequence could land and that the parent didn't intervene. They have noticed, possibly without words for it, that something in the quality of the parents' attention has shifted. And they are waiting. They are watching for when the shift reverses, when the pressure of a difficult situation or a spike of anxiety causes the parent to reach for the Closed Hand and confirm that nothing has really changed.

Every week, the parent maintains the Open Hand through the child's resistance, without requiring the child to acknowledge the change or reciprocate with warmth, adds to the body of evidence the child is building about whether this time is actually different. This is why the absence of a visible response is not evidence of no impact. The impact is occurring. It is occurring in the child's private assessment of whether the pattern has genuinely shifted — and that assessment is taking place behind the closed door, the monosyllable, and the edge in the voice, invisible to the parent who works so hard on the other side of it. Consistency without visible reward is the message that this time is different. It is the only message the child who has learned not to trust change will eventually believe.

12.4 Building Resilience for the Long Seasons

There are seasons in this work that are longer and harder than others. Seasons of sustained silence. Seasons where the progress of previous weeks seems to have evaporated. Seasons where the relationship contracts rather than expands, where the child seems further away rather than closer, where the anxiety returns at a volume that makes the deliberate choice feel almost impossibly hard.

These seasons are not failures of the framework. They are features of the terrain, and the parent who has been told in advance that they exist and given the specific practices for navigating them is far less likely to be undone by them. Here are the resilience practices that sustain open-handed parenting through the hardest stretches:

Return to the Evidence File

The Evidence File you have been building since the Loosen stage is most valuable precisely in the seasons when it feels least relevant — because the seasons when the child's capability is hardest to believe in are the seasons when the documented, specific, irrefutable record of that capability is most needed.

Return to it. Read it from the beginning. Notice that the entries are real, that each one represents when your child handled something without your intervention and showed a resilience or competence that the anxiety had been underestimating. Let the accumulation of those moments speak to the catastrophising loop with something the loop cannot easily dismiss: evidence.

Anchor to the Flourish Markers

Return to the specific, emotionally precise images you identified in Chapter 11. Not as a measure of how far you still have to go — on the hardest days, that measure will feel unbearable. As a reminder of why the current difficulty is worth sustaining.

The parent who can, in a tough season, access the specific felt image of the voluntary phone call, the Sunday dinner chosen freely, or the actual conversation that goes somewhere genuine has an anchor that anxiety cannot dislodge. Not because the image makes the current difficulty disappear. Because it keeps the destination visible when the progress feels invisible.

Use the Consistency Protocol as a Lifeline

In difficult seasons, the Consistency Protocol, the daily five-minute check-in, the weekly twenty-minute review, the monthly WALLS assessment, is not background maintenance. It is the lifeline.

The parent who maintains these practices through the hardest stretches is doing something that requires more discipline than any other element of the framework: they are choosing the relationship over the result, the practice over the payoff, the Open Hand over the reassurance of the Closed one, in the specific, sustained absence of visible reward. That choice, maintained across the tough season, is what transforms the framework from a set of practices into a lived identity. The parent who keeps showing up with an Open Hand when it is not being met is not failing. They are becoming.

Separate the Self From the Season

This is perhaps the most important resilience practice of all, and the one most easily lost in the thick of a hard stretch. The season's difficulty is not a measure of who you are. It is a measure of where the relationship currently is. Those are not the same thing. The parent who, in a difficult season, conflates the relationship's current state with their own worth as a parent is the parent most likely to reach for the Closed Hand — because the Closed Hand at least produces the feeling of doing something, of being in control of something, of mattering in a way that the Open Hand's patient, unrewarded consistency does not provide.

Write this down somewhere visible: *The season's difficulty is not a verdict on my worth. It is information about where the relationship is. And where the relationship is, right now, is inside the most important and least rewarded part of the transformation.*

12.5 The Truth About Timing

There is no timeline for this. No chapter of this book will tell you how long the silence will last, when the first voluntary contact will come, or how many consistent weeks of Open Hand parenting are required before a particular child begins to move toward a particular parent.

Because the timing is not the parent's to control. And the attempt to control it , to calculate, to strategise, to manage the pace of the child's response ,is the Closed Hand reaching into the one dimension of the relationship that most genuinely requires the Open Hand.

What the research says, consistently, across decades of attachment studies and relational repair literature, is this: the child who experiences a genuinely, sustainably changed parental pattern will, in almost all cases, eventually respond to it. Not always as the parent imagined. Not always on the timeline the parent hoped. But the human attachment bond, even when strained for years, retains a remarkable capacity for recovery.

The parent who keeps going when nothing seems to work is not failing the framework. They are the framework. They are the living proof, visible to a watching child, that the love being offered is no longer conditional on the response it receives. That proof, patient, consistent, unrewarded, is the most powerful thing available. And it is what changes everything.

The Resilience Practices at a Glance

Practice	When to Use It	What It Provides
The Rupture Recovery Tool	Within 24 hours of any old-pattern interaction	A three-step return to the framework—without shame, without spiral, with one specific forward commitment
Return to the Evidence File	In any season when the child's capability feels hardest to believe	The personal, specific, irrefutable record of capability that the catastrophising loop cannot easily dismiss
Anchor to the Flourish Markers	In any season when progress feels invisible	A specific, emotionally precise reminder of what the current difficulty is building toward
The Consistency Protocol as Lifeline	Through every difficult season, without exception	The sustained, visible, unrewarded Open Hand—the only message that convinces a watching child this time is different
Separate Self From Season	Whenever the relationship's current state is being mistaken for a verdict on parental worth	The clarity that the season's difficulty is information, not judgment—and that keeping going inside it is the most important work available

Table 12: Showing Resilience Practices at a Glance

Key Takeaway 12

The parent who keeps going when nothing seems to work **is not failing the framework; they are within the most important part of it.** Consistency in the absence of visible reward is the single most powerful signal a parent can send to a child who has learned not to trust that change is real. It is the proof that this time is different.

And proof, patient, specific, unrewarded, sustained, is what the child who has been managed for years is quietly waiting for, behind the closed door and the monosyllable and the edge in the voice. Keep going. Not because it is easy. Because it is the work. And because the parent who keeps going through this season is not just building a relationship with their child.

They are becoming someone their child will one day be proud to have returned to.

Chapter 13 addresses one of the most practically significant challenges in this transformation: the co-parenting relationship. Because the open-handed work you are doing does not happen in a vacuum. It happens inside a family, and the other adult in that family has a parenting approach, a set of beliefs about love and control, and a response to the changes you *make that will either support the transformation or create friction within it. Chapter 13 gives you the specific tools to navigate that dynamic, whether your partner is ready to join the journey, resistant to it, or somewhere in the uncertain territory between.*

Chapter Thirteen

The Co-Parent Conversation

No transformation that happens inside a family happens in isolation and the parent who has been doing this work while the other adult in their child's life continues to operate from an entirely different set of assumptions is navigating something that deserves its own chapter, its own honest examination, and its own specific tools.

This chapter is that examination. It is not a chapter about blame. The co-parent, whether a spouse, a separated partner, or any other adult who shares significant responsibility for your child's life, is not the obstacle to your transformation. They are, in almost every case, a person who loves your child as much as you do and who is parenting from the same fundamental drive that brought you to this book: the desire to get it right for someone they love deeply.

The fact that their approach may differ from the one you are building, sometimes significantly, sometimes in ways that create direct friction with the open-handed work you are doing, is not evidence of inadequacy on their part. It is evidence of the same thing that produced your own pattern: a set of inherited beliefs about love, safety, and control that were never examined with the honest, structured attention this book has been asking of you.

The question this chapter addresses is not whether your co-parent is parenting correctly. It is how you navigate the specific, practical challenge of doing open-handed work inside a relationship, with your child, and with your partner, when the other adult in the equation has not yet made the same shift.

13.1 The Three Co-Parenting Scenarios

Before we move on to the tools, it is worth naming the three most common scenarios that parents find themselves in when they arrive at this chapter, because the approach differs meaningfully depending on which one applies to you.

Scenario 1 — The Willing Partner. Your co-parent is open to the conversation. They may not have read this book, and they may not immediately embrace every element of the framework, but they are receptive to the idea that something needs to change and willing to engage with the language and concepts you bring to them. This is the easiest scenario to navigate, not without its challenges, but with the significant advantage of a shared direction.

Scenario 2 — The Resistant Partner. Your co-parent is sceptical, defensive, or actively resistant to the suggestion that the family's parenting approach needs to be examined. They may interpret the conversation as a critique of their parenting, specifically. They may have entrenched views about what good parenting looks like that differ significantly from the open-handed model. They may simply not be ready , for reasons that have nothing to do with the quality of their love for your child. This scenario requires patience, strategy, and the specific tools of the Partner Alignment Conversation, applied with the utmost care.

Scenario 3 — The Absent or Disengaged Partner. Your co-parent is not present, through separation, divorce, or simply a pattern of disengagement that has left you as the primary, effectively solo navigator of the parenting relationship. In this scenario, the co-parenting challenge is not about alignment with a partner but about managing the specific ways in which the absent or disengaged parent's behaviour affects the child and the open-handed work you are doing. Each scenario has its own navigation. We'll address them.

13.2 Scenario 1 — Bringing a Willing Partner Into the Framework

The willing partner is the easiest audience for the Partner Alignment Conversation — and the most common mistake parents make with them is treating their willingness as a license to move too fast.

The parent who has spent eight chapters building toward a complete understanding of the WALLS Framework is tempted, when they finally have a receptive co-parent in front of them, to deliver the full architecture in a single conversation. The Fear Audit.

The Three-Hand Method. The Deliberate Step Back. The Repair Conversation. All of it, enthusiastically and comprehensively, in one sitting.

The co-parent who receives this, however willing they are, is being handed the equivalent of 12 chapters of material they haven't read and asked to process it in real time. They cannot. And the gap between your depth of understanding and theirs, communicated in that single conversation, is likely to produce one of two unhelpful outcomes: they feel overwhelmed and quietly disengage, or they feel like a student receiving instruction from a teacher rather than a partner in a shared endeavour. Neither serves the transformation you're trying to build together.

The approach with a willing partner is slow, specific, and collaborative. Begin with one concept. Not the whole framework, but one concept. The Three-Hand Model is the most accessible entry point because it offers a language rather than a programme. You are not asking your partner to commit to a six-week transformation. You are offering them a way of talking about parenting moments that both of you might find useful.

Introduce it as a question rather than a teaching: *"I've been thinking about something, and I'd love to hear your take on it. I've started noticing that I* parent in *one of three modes, and I'm curious whether this resonates with you too."* Then describe the three hands. Without the full theoretical architecture. And invite their responses.

From that conversation, one of two things will happen: they will engage with the language and begin using it, or they will engage with it partially and need time to sit with it before it becomes genuinely useful to them. Either response is fine. Both are the beginning of a shared language rather than a taught programme, and shared language produces shared direction.

Move through the framework's concepts in this way, one at a time, introduced as conversations rather than lessons, received as collaborative inquiry rather than individual correction, and what you build is not a co-parent who has been persuaded to adopt your approach, but a partner who has arrived, through genuine engagement, at something that feels like their own. That quality of ownership sustains the alignment through the tough seasons.

13.3 Scenario 2 — Navigating a Resistant Partner

The resistant partner requires an entirely different approach, and it begins with reframing the goal of the conversation. The goal is not to convert. It is not to persuade your partner that the WALLS Framework is correct and their current approach is incorrect. It is not to produce agreement, or acknowledgement, or even understanding in a single conversation. The goal is to open a door. Just that. To create a small, non-threatening aperture through which a different conversation might eventually become possible.

Here is what makes resistance in a co-parent so understandable, and so important to hold with compassion rather than frustration. The parent who is resistant to the suggestion that their parenting approach needs examination is, in almost all cases, a parent for whom that approach is deeply connected to their identity, values, or inherited understanding of what it means to love and protect a child.

When you introduce the concepts of this book to a resistant partner, you are not just offering a different parenting framework. You are, from their perspective, suggesting that the framework through which they have been expressing their love for your child is inadequate. That is not a neutral suggestion. And the defensiveness it produces is not unreasonable.

The approach with a resistant partner has three non-negotiable principles:

Principle 1 — Lead With the Relationship, Not the Framework

Never begin the conversation with the framework. Begin with the relationship specifically with a shared observation about the child and the relationship, expressed as concern rather than critique. Not: *"I've been reading this book, and I think we need to change how we parent."*

Instead: *"I've been thinking a lot about [child's name] lately. I feel like there's some distance between us that I want to address, and I'm wondering if you've noticed the same thing."* Almost all co-parents, whatever their parenting philosophy, share the underlying goal of a close, healthy relationship with their child. Starting from that shared goal, from the concern rather than the solution, creates the conditions for a conversation that both parties can enter without one of them feeling immediately positioned as the problem.

Principle 2 — Share Your Own Journey, Not Their Diagnosis

The most important thing you can offer a resistant partner is not the framework. It is your own honest account of what you have discovered about yourself through this work. Not: *"I think you operate from the Closed Hand a lot."* Instead: *"I've realised that a lot of what I thought was good parenting has actually been driven by my own anxiety — and that some of it has been creating distance rather than closeness. That's been a difficult thing to see. But it's also been really useful."*

When you speak from your own experience rather than your partner's, you remove the defensiveness trigger. You are no longer diagnosing them; you are sharing something vulnerable about yourself. And vulnerability, offered genuinely, tends to invite reciprocity rather than resistance.

Your partner may not immediately respond with their own self-reflection. But the conversation has been positioned as one between two people with a shared investment in something important — rather than one between a parent who has figured something out and a partner who needs to catch up.

Principle 3 — Offer Language, Not a Programme

As with the willing partner, the entry point for the resistant one is a concept rather than a curriculum. But with a resistant partner, the concept needs to be even simpler and even less prescriptive.

The Three-Hand Model, introduced as a casual observation rather than a framework presentation, is often the most accessible: *"I've started trying to notice, at the moment, whether I'm responding from fear or from trust. It's harder than it sounds, but I've found it really useful. Does that distinction resonate with you at all?"* An open question. Genuine curiosity about their responses. No investment in a particular answer. The resistant partner who is given language rather than a programme, and a question rather than an expectation, has something they can engage with on their own terms. And engagement on their own terms, however partial, however tentative, is the beginning of movement.

13.4 Scenario 3 — Parenting Effectively When Alignment Is Absent

For the parent who is navigating this work without a co-parent or with one whose level of disengagement or conflict makes the alignment conversation currently impossible the question is not how to bring a partner into the framework but how to sustain open-handed parenting when the family environment does not consistently support it. This is genuinely hard. And it deserves an honest acknowledgement of that hardness before any tools are offered. The child who experiences consistent Open Hand parenting from one parent and Closed Hand parenting from the other is receiving mixed signals about the relationship between love and control. The open-handed work you are doing with them will not be undermined by this; children can hold different relationship qualities with different adults, but it will sometimes be complicated by it. The child who has been allowed a natural consequence by one parent and had it reversed by the other has received a mixed message about trust that will take longer to process than the same consequence consistently applied. You cannot control what happens in the other parent's interactions with your child. What you can control is the consistency and quality of your own, and that consistency, sustained across the full range of your parenting interactions, regardless of what is happening in the co-parenting relationship, is what your child will build their trust in.

Here are the specific practices for the parent navigating this without alignment:

Maintain the Consistency Protocol regardless of co-parenting conditions. The daily check-in, the weekly review, and the monthly WALLS assessment do not depend on your co-parent's participation. They are yours, and their value is entirely independent of whether the other adult in your child's life is doing parallel work.

Resist the temptation to position yourself as the open-handed alternative to your co-parent's closed one. The parent who, consciously or unconsciously, allows their open-handed approach to become defined in contrast to their partner's closed one is introducing a triangulation dynamic into the relationship that will not serve the child. Your Open Hand is not a correction of the other parent's Closed one. It is simply the way you are choosing to love your child — offered on its own terms, without reference to any comparison.

Use the Repair Conversation to address any confusion the mixed signals have created. If your child has been receiving significantly different parenting from two adults

and seems confused or caught between them, a version of the Repair Conversation —
adapted to name only your own approach, without reference to or criticism of the other
parent, can provide valuable clarity. *"I want you to know what you can expect from me. I'm
working on being someone you can come to with the real stuff. I will not manage your life —
I'm going to be present in it. That's what I'm building. It's yours whenever you want it."*

13.5 The WALLS Framework Applied to the Partnership Itself

Here is something this chapter has been building toward that is worth naming explicitly.

The same principles that are rebuilding your relationship with your child apply, without exception, to your co-parenting relationship.

The partner who is resistant to the Partner Alignment Conversation is not so different
from the child who resists the Repair Conversation. Both are people who have developed,
through accumulated experience, a set of protective responses to the dynamics of this
relationship. Both require the same thing from you: changed behaviour sustained over
time, offered without demand for immediate reciprocity, demonstrated through consistent action rather than single conversations.

The Open Question practice works in the co-parenting relationship as powerfully as
it works in the parent-child one. *"What do you think has been happening between us and
[child's name] lately?"* is an Open Question. *"What would feel most supportive to you in
how we handle this together?"* is an Open Question. Genuine curiosity about your partner's experience, asked without an agenda, received without redirecting, creates the same
relational conditions in the partnership that it creates in the parent-child relationship.

The Deliberate Step Back works in the co-parenting relationship, too. The parent who
would ordinarily step in to manage a situation between their partner and their child,
correcting, redirecting, or softening the other parent's approach, and who instead holds
the Open Hand, is practising the same discipline in the adult relationship that the Loosen
stage asked of them in the parent-child one.

And the Repair Conversation, offered to a partner, not a child, but with the same three
elements and the same release of outcome — can open a door in the co-parenting relationship that no amount of strategic alignment conversation has opened. The framework
is not limited to a single relationship. It is a way of loving. And it works wherever love is
present, and fear has been driving.

The Co-Parent Navigation at a Glance

Scenario	Primary Challenge	Key Approach
Willing Partner	Moving too fast, overwhelming with the full framework	Slow, specific, collaborative—one concept at a time, introduced as shared inquiry
Resistant Partner	Triggering defensiveness by positioning them as the problem	Lead with relationship not framework, share your journey not their diagnosis, offer language, not programme
Absent or Misaligned Partner	Sustaining open-handed parenting without co-parenting support	Maintain Consistency Protocol independently, avoid triangulation, use Repair Conversation for child-facing clarity
The Partnership Itself	Forgetting that the WALLS Framework applies to adult relationships too	Open Questions, Deliberate Step Back, and Repair Conversation all transfer directly to the co-parenting dynamic

Table 13: Showing Co-Parent Navigation at a Glance

Key Takeaway 13

The co-parenting dimension is not a sidebar to this transformation; **it is one of its most practically significant dimensions.** The parent who brings their partner into the WALLS Framework journey, however imperfectly, multiplies the transformation's reach into every relationship within the family. And the parent who navigates the co-parenting challenge alone, with consistency, without triangulation, and with the same open-handed principles they are bringing to the parent-child relationship, discovers that unilateral change, sustained over time, creates the conditions that make everything else more possible.

The co-parenting relationship is not a separate problem to be solved alongside the transformation. It is part of the transformation. And the tools you already have are precisely the ones it requires.

Chapter 14 takes the framework into the specific, often more painful, terrain of the adult child,, the son or daughter who is no longer a teenager navigating development but an adult navigating a relationship with a parent whose pattern has been operating, sometimes, *for decades. The distance in these relationships can feel more calcified, more permanent, more resistant to the change this framework describes. Chapter 14 addresses that specific fear directly and offers both the evidence and the adapted practices that make open-handed love as available to the parent of a 28-year-old as to the parent of a 15-year-old.*

There is no age at which this work becomes irrelevant. And Chapter 14 is where you'll discover exactly why.

Chapter Fourteen

Loving the Adult Child You Didn't Expect

The fear that arrives most powerfully in the parent of an adult child is not the fear that the relationship is difficult. It is the fear that the relationship is finished , that the distance has been in place long enough and has hardened sufficiently, that the word repair no longer applies to it.

That fear has a name. It is called *too late*. And it is the fear this chapter is written specifically to dismantle. Not with false reassurance. Not with the vague, consoling claim that it's never too late, with no evidence to support it. But with the specific, research-grounded, story-substantiated truth that the parent-child attachment bond, even after years of significant distance, even after patterns of interaction that both parties regard as permanent, even after the relationship has contracted to the point of holidays and obligatory calls and the particular ache of a closeness that once existed and has never been recovered, keeps a capacity for transformation that the fear of *too late* consistently and dramatically underestimates.

You may be the parent of a 22-year-old whose life choices you still struggle to let go of. Or the parent of a 25-year-old whose relationship with you carries the quality of an obligation rather than a choice. Or the parent of a 28-year-old whose distance has settled into a pattern that both of you have, perhaps without fully realising it, treated as the relationship's permanent shape.

This chapter is for all of you. Because the framework you have been building across the chapters behind you has no age limit. And the open-handed love it asks of you is, if anything, more available, not less, when the child receiving it is an adult.

14.1 What Changes With an Adult Child — and What Doesn't

The parent-child relationship changes significantly when the child reaches adulthood. The daily logistics that once structured the relationship — the school run, the homework, the dinner table, the bedtime — are gone. The physical proximity that once made connection incidental rather than deliberate has contracted. The natural, frequent, low-stakes interactions that used to constitute the fabric of the relationship have been replaced by something more intentional, more occasional, and — when the relationship has been strained — more fraught.

What changes, in practical terms, is the terrain. The situations that call for open-handed parenting are no longer the homework essay, the friendship conflict, or the missed curfew. They are the career decisions you disagree with. The relationship you are concerned about. The lifestyle choices that diverge from your values in ways that are difficult to watch. The specific, adult-terrain moments where the Closed Hand reaches for involvement that is no longer yours to offer.

What does not change is the underlying dynamic. The fear beneath the grip is the same fear. The grief beneath the anxiety is the same grief. The message that the Closed Hand sends to an adult child — *I don't trust you to handle your own life* — lands with the same relational weight it has always carried, and produces, many times, the same response: a gradual, self-protective withdrawal from the parent who makes them feel managed rather than trusted.

The adult child who has been pulling away from a managing parent is not doing something that requires a fundamentally different framework. They are doing the same thing the teenager was doing, for the same reasons, in a more visible and more autonomous form.

Which means the same framework applies. Adapted, yes. Calibrated to the adult terrain, certainly. But built on exactly the same principles, because the principles are not specific to a developmental stage. They are specific to love and what happens when fear speaks louder than love.

14.2 The Specific Challenges of the Adult Child Relationship

Before we adapt the framework's tools for the adult terrain, it is worth naming the specific challenges that make this relationship feel harder than the parent-teenager dynamic in certain important respects.

The distance is often more entrenched. The teenager's distance is developmental; it has a trajectory, a natural arc, a biological programme that, most times, moves toward eventual re-engagement. The adult child's distance has no such built-in arc. It can calcify. It can become the relationship's established mode, maintained not through hostility but through a kind of polite, managed, surface-level contact that neither party challenges because both parties have quietly given up on something deeper.

The leverage points are fewer. The parent of a teenager has natural, regular points of contact, the family dinner, the car journey, the ordinary domestic interactions that create the opportunity for the Repair Conversation and the Open Question practice. The parent of an adult child who lives independently has the interactions they actively create, and creating them, when the relationship has contracted to a pattern of infrequent contact, requires a quality of intentionality that the parent-teenager relationship does not.

The shame of the long duration. The parent whose adult child has been distant for years carries not just the grief of the distance but the specific, compounding shame of its duration. The longer it has gone on, the harder it is to believe that change is possible — and the more the shame of having let it continue feeds the fear of trying and failing, making the distance permanent rather than potentially bridgeable.

The adult child's autonomy is non-negotiable. The teenager's autonomy is developing the parent still has a degree of structural influence over the relationship's conditions. The adult child's autonomy is complete. They choose at every point whether to engage with the parents' attempts to change the relationship's dynamic. They cannot be required to attend the family dinner. They cannot be expected to respond to the Open Question if they have decided, based on years of experience, that engaging with their parent's questions carries costs they are no longer willing to pay.

These challenges are real. None of them makes the transformation impossible. But all of them require honest acknowledgement, because the parent who approaches the adult child relationship with the same timeline expectations they might have for the parent-teenager relationship will be disappointed by the pace of it, and may interpret that slower pace as evidence that the work isn't functioning when it is, in fact, functioning exactly as it should.

14.3 How the Framework Adapts for the Adult Child

The WALLS Framework applies in full to the adult-child relationship. But several of its practices require specific adaptation to function effectively in this terrain.

Adapting the Fear Audit

The Fear Audit for the parent of an adult child looks different from the version you completed in Chapter 7. The ten most frequent Closed Hand interventions are not the essay rewrite and the follow-up text, they are the comment about the career choice, the question about the relationship that is really a concern in question form, the unsolicited advice offered in the brief window of a phone call, the opinion shared about a life decision that is no longer the parent's to influence.

Complete the Fear Audit again, but this time populate it specifically with the adult-terrain interventions. The ones that happen in the interactions you have, and notice, particularly, the ones that happen in your mind in the interactions you don't have. Because the parent of an adult child often runs the Closed Hand not just in the conversations, they have but in the mental rehearsal of conversations that haven't happened yet, pre-loading the interaction with the anxious assessment of what needs to be said, what needs to be managed, what the adult child needs to understand.

That mental Closed Hand is as much a part of the pattern as the spoken one. And naming it in the Fear Audit gives you something to work with in the Three-Second Check before the conversation has even begun.

Adapting the Deliberate Step Back

The Deliberate Step Back for the parent of an adult child is most commonly the decision not to say the thing that the anxiety is making them want to say. Not the intervention in a physical situation, the adult child is not arriving home at 2 am or submitting an assignment. The intervention is verbal, opinionated, and advisory. It is a comment about a relationship partner that is offered as concern but received as criticism. It is the question about the job situation that is asked out of genuine worry, but experienced as monitoring. It is the unsolicited advice about a financial decision, a health choice, or a lifestyle pattern that the parent finds difficult to watch.

The Deliberate Step Back, in this context, is the choice to hold the Open Hand in the conversation rather than the Closed one. To ask a genuine question instead of making a concerned observation. To listen to the adult child's account of their own life without the commentary that turns listening into managing.

Apply the Three-Question Reflection after each such step back, in exactly the same way as the Chapter 9 version, because the gap between the feared outcome (the adult child makes a terrible decision without your input) and the actual outcome (the adult child continues to make their own decisions, as they always have, with or without your commentary) is, many times, as wide and as instructive in the adult relationship as it is in the teenage one.

Adapting the Repair Conversation

The Repair Conversation for the adult-child relationship carries the same three elements as the version in Chapter 10, but it is offered in a different register because the adult child brings to the conversation a longer history and a more fully developed capacity to assess the sincerity of what they're hearing.

The adult child who has been managing a difficult relationship with a parent for years has, most times, a sophisticated internal model of that parent's behaviour. They know the patterns. They have developed, necessarily, as self-protection, a reliable ability to distinguish between a genuine shift and a temporary adjustment, between a parent who has changed and a parent who is trying harder in the same direction as before.

The Repair Conversation with an adult child must therefore be accompanied by the most honest possible acknowledgement of duration. Not only do *I see what has been happening between us*, but *I see that it has been happening for a long time, and that* the time *is part of what I am acknowledging.*

Here is the adapted version of the three elements for the adult child relationship:

"I can see what has been happening between us, and I can see that it has been happening for longer than I have been willing to honestly acknowledge."

"I am working on changing my part in it, not as a temporary change, but as a genuine shift in how I understand my role in your life and in our relationship."

"I am not asking you to respond to this, and I am not asking you to trust it immediately. I am simply showing you something different — and I am going to keep showing it, for as long as it takes, because you deserve it and because the relationship we could have is worth more than my discomfort with the pace of it."

The third element, the release of outcome, is critical in the adult-child relationship because the adult child's response to the Repair Conversation is far less predictable than the teenager's. Some adult children will receive it with immediate and visible emotion. Some will receive it with polite acknowledgement and no apparent change. Some will not acknowledge it at all in the moment — and will process it privately, over weeks or months, in ways that eventually produce a shift that the parent could not have expected from the initial response.

Release the outcome. Completely. Not as a strategy for producing a better response, but as a genuine surrender of the need for the conversation to land the way you intended it to. The gift is in the offering. What the adult child does with it is theirs to determine.

Adapting the Consistency Protocol

The Consistency Protocol for the adult child relationship requires an additional layer of intentionality because the natural, frequent, low-stakes contact points that make the protocol relatively straightforward in the parent-teenager relationship do not exist in the same way.

The daily five-minute check-in, in this context, is not a nightly conversation; it is a commitment to the quality of presence you bring to whatever contact occurs. One genuine, Open Question-structured interaction per point of contact. Not every day, but every interaction, however infrequent, is governed by the Open Hand and the genuine curiosity that makes contact feel like connection rather than obligation.

The weekly twenty-minute review remains as described in Chapter 10, adapted to the adult terrain by focusing not on daily interactions but on the quality and texture of the week's contact, however limited it was.

And the monthly WALLS assessment gains an additional dimension for the parent of an adult child: an explicit, honest assessment of whether the level of contact is being maintained. Not monitored with the anxious frequency of the Closed Hand, but protected with the deliberate, consistent intention of a parent who has decided that the relationship is worth showing up for, even when showing up is met with minimal reciprocation.

14.4 The "It Is Already Too Late" Objection

This chapter has been building toward this moment since its first paragraph. Because the fear of being *too late* is not just an occasional concern for the parent of an adult child, it is often the primary reason they have not already attempted the work this framework asks of them.

And it deserves a direct, honest, evidence-based response.

The attachment research, from Bowlby's foundational work through the most recent longitudinal studies of adult parent-child relationships, is consistent on one point that the fear of being *too late* consistently ignores: the parent-child attachment bond does not have an expiry date.

This does not mean that every estranged relationship can be fully repaired, or that every adult child who has created significant distance will eventually move back toward the parent who changes. Some relationships have sustained damage that requires professional support beyond what any book can provide. Some adult children have built lives and identities at a sufficient distance from the parenting relationship that the pace of change will be genuinely slow.

But the research is equally consistent on a second point: the parent who genuinely, demonstrably, and sustainably changes their pattern of relating — who offers the open-handed love of the WALLS Framework with real consistency over real time, produces a change in the relational dynamic in the vast majority of cases studied. Not always dramatic. Not always fast. But real, and measurable, and toward the relationship both parties have, beneath the distance and the grief and the fear of too late, always wanted.

The door is not locked from the outside. It is not even locked. It is simply closed, and the parent who keeps showing up at it, with an open hand and no demand for immediate entry, is the parent who discovers, eventually, that it opens. The timeline is not yours to control. The showing up i

Ts.

The Adult Child Adaptations at a Glance

Framework Tool	Standard Version	Adult Child Adaptation
Fear Audit	Ten most frequent Closed Hand interventions in daily parenting	Adult-terrain interventions named—verbal, advisory, and the mental Closed Hand in pre-conversation rehearsal
Deliberate Step Back	Choosing not to physically intervene in a situation	Choosing not to offer the comment, advice, or concerned question that the anxiety is making you want to say
Repair Conversation	Three elements with the release of the outcome	Same three elements, adapted to acknowledge duration explicitly and release outcome with specific awareness of the adult child's longer processing timeline
Consistency Protocol	Daily check-in, weekly review, monthly assessment	Quality of presence in each point of contact, rather than frequency; intentional maintenance of contact level

Table 14: Showing Adult-Child Adaptations at a Glance

Key Takeaway 14

There is no age at which this work becomes irrelevant. The adult child who has been pulling away for years is not gone; they are waiting, with the same fragile hope their parent carries, for evidence that the relationship can be something different. Open-handed love, offered consistently and without agenda, has an extraordinary record of reopening doors that fear had convinced both parties were permanently closed.

It is not too late. It has never been too late. And the parent who begins this work today, with a 22-year-old, a 25-year-old, or a 28-year-old who has been quietly waiting for exactly this , is beginning it at precisely the right moment. The right moment is always now.

Chapter 15 turns toward the specific situation that produces the most acute anxiety for any parent attempting this work: *the teenager who is not withdrawing quietly, but actively, sometimes* hostile, *pushing back against every open-handed attempt the parent makes. The door is not just closed in this relationship. It sometimes feels like it is being held shut from the other side.*

What the research reveals about that teenager, and what the parent who stays open-handed through the hostility ultimately discovers, is one of the most counterintuitive and important truths in this entire book. Chapter 15 is where you find it.

The Teenager Who Won't Talk to You

The hostile teenager is not proof that the framework does not work. They are proof that the parents' previous approach has been deeply felt. That distinction between a framework that has failed and a child who has noticed is the entire foundation of this chapter. And it is a distinction that requires a quality of nerve that no other situation in this book asks of you so directly, because the hostile teenager does not make it easy to hold. They make it feel, on the days when the contempt is loudest and the silence most impenetrable, like the opposite of that distinction is true.

They make it feel like nothing is working. Like the Open Hand is being actively refused. Like the Repair Conversation landed in empty space. As if every Open Question is met with a response designed specifically to communicate that the question was not welcome, that the parent is not welcome, and that the entire project of rebuilding this relationship is not welcome.

On those days, and they will come, for the parent of a genuinely hostile or withdrawn teenager, this chapter is the one you return to. Not because it makes the hostility easier to bear. But because it gives it a meaning that the fear, left unchecked, would never arrive at on its own.

15.1 Understanding the Hostile Teenager

There is a clinical observation that runs through decades of adolescent psychology research, and that is, in the experience of every practitioner who works with this population, consistently and reliably true: **The teenager who is most hostile is almost always the one who is most closely watching.** Not watching from a position of indifference. Watching from a position of guarded, self-protective, deeply conditioned vigilance, the vigilance of a person who has been managed for long enough that they have developed a sophisticated ability to detect the difference between a parent who is genuinely changing and a parent who is trying harder in the same direction as before.

The hostility is not indifference wearing an aggressive mask. It is an investment wearing a defensive one. The teenager who does not care has not developed a defensive posture toward the parent's attempts to reconnect; they have simply disengaged. The teenager who is actively hostile, who responds to the Open Question with contempt and to the Repair Conversation with a closed door, is paying close attention. They are testing. Not consciously, not strategically, they are not running a deliberate programme of evaluation. But at a level below conscious decision, they are asking the question that their history with this parent has taught them to ask: *Is this real? Will it last? Or will it* revert *under* pressure *to the pattern I already know?*

The hostility is the test. And the parent who holds the Open Hand through the hostility, who does not retreat into the Closed Hand in response to the contempt, who does not withdraw the genuine curiosity of the Open Question because it was met with a shrug or a sneer, is the parent who is passing the test. Not because passing it produces an immediate reward. But because the teenager who is watching most closely will eventually register that this parent is not reverting. That registration, private, and never acknowledged in the moment it occurs, is what shifts the relationship.

15.2 Why the Closed Hand Makes Things Worse Here?

The temptation when facing a hostile teenager is to match the energy. Not with hostility, most parents are past that, but with pressure. With the escalated version of the Closed Hand that produces confrontations, ultimatums, and the specific interaction that feels, at the moment, like it might finally break through the wall. It doesn't. And understanding why it doesn't, specifically and mechanically, not just as an abstract principle, is what gives the parent the grounding to resist the temptation in the moments when it is strongest.

The hostile teenager's nervous system is, in the language of neuroscience, in a state of defensive arousal. The adolescent brain, as Daniel Siegel's research on this population makes clear, is already characterised by heightened sensitivity to perceived threat, heightened reactivity to social dynamics, and a significantly reduced capacity for the prefrontal processing that allows for rational, calm, considered response to an adult's input.

When that brain, already operating at elevated reactivity, encounters a parent whose own anxiety is rising in response to the hostility, whose questions are coming faster, whose voice has taken on the particular quality of urgent need that the Closed Hand produces under pressure, it does not experience this as an invitation to engage. It experiences it as a threat. And the response to a threat, in an adolescent nervous system already primed for defensive arousal, is more hostility, deeper withdrawal, or the specific contemptuous dismissal designed, above all else, to end the interaction and remove the source of perceived pressure.

The Closed Hand, applied to a hostile teenager, does not produce a connection. It produces the exact dynamic it was trying to prevent. The Open Hand, held steadily, without pressure, without urgent need for a response, does something different. It does not remove the hostile teenager's defensive posture overnight. But it stops adding to it. And in the absence of an additional threat, defensive arousal gradually decreases over time with consistent exposure to a genuinely unique quality of parental presence. That lowering is not visible at first. But it is happening. And the parent who knows this, who has the neurological understanding to hold the Open Hand through periods when the lowering is invisible— is the parent who eventually sees it surface.

15.3 Adapting the Open Question Practice for the Hostile Teenager

The Open Question practice, as described in Chapter 10, produces its best results with a teenager who is withdrawn rather than actively hostile — a teenager who is not engaging but who is not, in the question's moment, actively refusing engagement.

For the hostile teenager, the standard Open Question structures require specific adaptation. Because the hostile teenager has, many times, developed a highly sensitised response to being asked questions by their parent, an automatic, almost Pavlovian interpretation of parental questioning as the opening move of a management interaction rather than a genuine act of curiosity.

The standard *"What was the best part of today?"* is not a neutral question for this teenager. It is a question that has been asked before in a hundred previous interactions, as a prelude to extracting information that the parent then used to direct, advise, or intervene. The hostile teenager knows this. And they respond not to the question as asked but to the question as they have learned to hear it — not as genuine curiosity but as the first move in a familiar game they have no interest in playing. The adapted Open Question practice for the hostile teenager has three specific modifications:

Modification 1: Lower the stakes of the question radically.

Not *"What's been on your mind lately?"* — that question carries too much emotional weight for the hostile teenager to receive without activating a defensive posture. Instead, the lowest-possible-stakes question. The most genuinely trivial question you can honestly ask — something about food, about something you observed together, about an entirely non-emotionally charged practical matter.

The purpose is not to build a deep connection through the question itself. The purpose is to create an interaction that does not trigger a defensive response — to establish that your question does not inevitably lead to a management interaction. That normalisation, built through dozens of low-stakes exchanges over time, gradually reconditions the hostile teenager's interpretation of parental questions.

Modification 2: Remove the expectation of a response.

The hostile teenager can hear the expectation in a question. Not the words, but the quality of waiting that follows them. The parent who asks a question and then stands in the room with their Open Hand visibly extended and their attention expectantly directed is communicating a need for response that the hostile teenager experiences as pressure, and responds to with exactly the defensive posture the question was trying to lower.

Ask the question in passing. Not as the centrepiece of a dedicated connection attempt, as a comment made in the flow of an ordinary domestic moment. *"I saw something on the way* home; *I thought you might find it funny."* And then tell it, or not, but without the weighted pause that signals the parent actually wanted engagement rather than exchange.

The question without the expectation is experienced entirely differently from the question with it. And the teenager who sees questions from their parent as genuinely low-stakes, as things that do not require a performance or prompt a management interaction, gradually becomes less hostile to being asked them.

Modification 3: Prioritise presence over connection.

The hostile teenager is not ready for the connection that the Open Question practice is ultimately designed to produce. They are not ready to bring their true selves into an exchange with the parent who has been managing that self for years. And asking them to do so, however gently, however genuinely, before the conditions for it have been built, is asking for something they are not yet safe enough to offer.

Prioritise being in the room without an agenda. Without a connection goal. Without the Open Hand extended in the obvious, effortful way that the hostile teenager reads as pressure. Being there, present, warm, unhurried, and making no demand on the quality of the interaction, is itself a practice. And it is the practice that lays the groundwork for everything the Open Question structure produces.

15.4 Adapting the Three-Hand Method for the Hostile Teenager

The Three-Second Check, in the hostile teenager, requires one specific addition to the standard three-step sequence. After Name the Hand, Check the Driver, and Choose the Hand; there is a fourth step that this context makes essential: **Check the Need.**

Specifically: *"Am I reaching for the Open Hand because it is genuinely the right response to this moment, or am I reaching for it because I need this interaction to go well and the Open Hand is what I have been told will make it go well?"*

This distinction matters more with the hostile teenager than with any other application of the framework, because the hostile teenager is exquisitely sensitive to the difference between a parent who is genuinely present and a parent who is performing presence in the service of an outcome they need.

The Open Hand held out of genuine trust is experienced differently by the teenager who is watching closely from the Open Hand held as a strategy for producing connection. The former is safe. The latter is, from the teenager's perspective, still the Closed Hand in different clothing — still a parent who needs something from them, whose behaviour is still about the parent's anxiety rather than the child's experience.

The Check the Need step interrupts that dynamic before it begins. It asks the parent to be honest about their driver, not just Fear versus Care, but Need versus Presence, and to choose the Open Hand only when the choice is coming from the latter.

When the choice is coming from the former, when the parent is honest with themselves, would admit that they need this interaction to go well, that they need the teenager to respond, that the Open Hand is being held with an urgency that is really the Closed Hand's anxiety wearing a different costume, the right response is not to continue. It is time to step back. To take a breath. To return when the presence is genuine rather than strategic. The hostile teenager will wait. The genuine presence, when it arrives, will be worth waiting for.

15.5 The Repair Conversation With a Hostile Teenager

The Repair Conversation with a hostile teenager is the highest-stakes application of this practice in the entire framework. And it requires, more than any other version of it, the absolute, uncompromising release of outcome that Chapter 10 described.

Because the hostile teenager's response to the Repair Conversation may not just be silence or minimal acknowledgement. It may be contempt. It may be a response that is specifically designed, whether consciously or not — to destabilise the parent's attempt at genuine vulnerability. To test, with maximum pressure, whether the change being offered is real.

Here is the specific guidance for delivering the Repair Conversation to a hostile teenager:

Choose the moment carefully. Not in the middle of a conflict. Not as a response to hostility, because a Repair Conversation delivered in reaction to the teenager's difficult behaviour will be heard as a tactic rather than a genuine offering. Choose a neutral moment. A car journey is often the most accessible — the side-by-side physical arrangement removes the face-to-face intensity that makes vulnerable conversations feel more exposing, and the built-in endpoint of the journey removes the pressure of open-ended duration.

Deliver it briefly. The three elements *I see in what has been* happening: *I am working on my part in it; I am not asking you to respond* — should be delivered in under two minutes. Not elaborated. Not explained. Not supported with examples or context, or the rich background of understanding you have built across this book. Two minutes. Three sentences. And then silence.

Expect nothing and mean it. The hostile teenager who receives a Repair Conversation and responds with contempt or dismissal is not telling you it didn't land. They are testing whether it will land differently — whether this parent, unlike the previous version of this parent, can say something vulnerable with no need for the vulnerability to be received in a particular way. Hold that. Do not qualify the three sentences with a fourth that seeks acknowledgement. Do not, in the days that follow, refer to the conversation or ask whether the teenager has thought about it. Deliver it. Release it. And let it do its work in the private space where the teenager who is watching closely is actually processing it.

15.6 What the Research Says About Hostile Teenagers and Relational Repair

The research on adolescent relational repair, across decades of attachment studies, family systems research, and longitudinal studies of parent-teenager relationship trajectories, supports one consistent finding that is worth delivering here without qualification.

The teenager who presents as most hostile toward a parent's attempts at genuine connection is, in most studied cases, the teenager who experiences the most profound shift when those attempts are sustained with genuine consistency over time.

Not because hostility is secretly enthusiasm in disguise. But because the depth of the defensive posture is a reliable indicator of the depth of the attachment wound, and the depth of the attachment wound is, paradoxically, a reliable indicator of the depth of the attachment bond that remains beneath it.

The teenager who is genuinely indifferent does not need to be hostile. The teenager who has fully detached does not require a defensive posture; there is nothing left to defend. The hostility, painful as it is to experience from the parent side, is evidence that the bond is still present and still felt. It is simply felt, right now, as pain rather than connection.

Open-handed parenting, applied consistently and without the demand for immediate reciprocity, has a documented and reliable record of reaching that bond — not by breaking through the defensive posture with sufficient force, but by being present for long enough, and genuinely enough, that the defensive posture gradually no longer serves its original purpose.

The hostile teenager who eventually opens a door to a changed parent is not doing something unexpected. They are doing exactly what the research predicted they would do, on exactly the timeline the research suggested they would need. The parents' job is to be there when it happens. Still open-handed. Still genuinely curious. Still present without an agenda. Still there.

The Hostile Teenager Adaptations at a Glance

Framework Tool	Standard Application	Hostile Teenager Adaptation
Open Question Practice	Five structures deployed with genuine curiosity	Radically lowered stakes, removed expectation of response, presence prioritised over connection
Three-Hand Method	Three-step check: Name, Driver, Choose	Four-step check: Name, Driver, Choose, plus Check the Need—distinguishing genuine presence from strategic performance
Repair Conversation	Three elements, released outcome	Brief delivery (under two minutes), car journey or side-by-side setting, zero reference in subsequent days
Consistency Protocol	Daily check-in, weekly review, monthly assessment	Maintained regardless of hostile response—the consistency IS the message, particularly when it is unrewarded

Table 15: Showing Hostile Teenager Adaptation at a Glance

Key Takeaway 15

The resistant teenager is not proof that the framework does not work. They are the proof that the parents' previous approach has been deeply felt — and that genuine, sustained change will be equally deeply felt. The parent who stays open-handed through the hostility is not losing. They are doing the most important work available to them at the most important moment in the relationship.

The hostile teenager is watching. They are testing. They are asking, in the only language currently available to them, whether this time is actually different. The answer is not delivered in words. It is delivered in the sustained, consistent, unrewarded presence of a parent who has decided, not because the response is encouraging, not because the relationship is easy, but because the love is real and the change is genuine — to keep showing up with an open hand. That answer, delivered often enough and held long enough, will be heard. It always is.

Chapter 16 brings the focus back to the parent, specifically to the full arc of the Identity Reclamation journey and what the parent discovers when they genuinely inhabit a life that is theirs. Because the parent who has walked through every stage of the WALLS Framework, navigated the difficult applications of Chapters 12 through 15, and sustained the open-handed approach through the hardest seasons has done something that deserves to be fully received: they have become someone different. Chapter 16 is where you meet that person — and discover that they were always who you were building toward.

Reclaiming the Parent You Always Meant to Be

There is a version of you that existed before the fear got loud, before the anxiety became the operating system, before the role consumed the person, before the love that was always enormous began expressing itself in ways that pushed away the very child it was trying to hold.

That version of you did not disappear. They were not erased by the intensive parenting years or dismantled by the pattern you have been working so hard to change. They have been present throughout, sometimes glimpsed in the rare, unguarded moments when the fear was quiet, and the love was simply itself, unfiltered by the anxiety that has been speaking louder than it for too long.

This chapter is where you meet that version of yourself again. Not as a recovery of something lost, you have lost nothing that cannot be reclaimed. But as the full, deliberate, finally resourced arrival at the person you were always building toward: the parent whose identity is whole enough, whose life is full enough, and whose love is open-handed enough that the relationship with their child becomes the richest thread in a rich fabric rather than the only thread in an empty one.

That parent is not different from the person who opened this book. They are the same person, finally free from the fear that has been speaking louder than their love for years. This is the chapter where they step forward.

16.1 The Full Identity Reclamation Arc

In Chapter 11, you began the Identity Reclamation Practice, a four-week, structured investment in one area of personal passion or interest that belongs entirely to you outside the parenting role. You named the thing. You invested the first hour. You began the expansion. You committed to integrating it permanently.

Chapter 16 is where that initial investment becomes something larger: the complete, comprehensive vision of who you are becoming in this next chapter of your life.

Not just the hobby reclaimed, or the interest re-engaged. The full identity, the person whose sense of self is distributed across multiple dimensions of meaning, contribution, passion, and relationship rather than concentrated entirely within a single role that has been slowly contracting as the child inside it has been growing up and away. This is the transformation that the Soar stage was always pointing toward. And it deserves, here at the close of the book's applied work, to be received in its full significance rather than treated as a supplementary self-care addendum to the actual work of relational repair. Because it is not supplementary. It is central. And the research supporting this is worth presenting with the specificity it deserves.

16.2 What the Research Says About Parental Identity and Relational Quality

The research on parental identity — on the relationship between a parent's sense of self outside the parenting role and the quality of the parent-child relationship — is consistent across multiple decades and multiple methodological approaches:

The parent who maintains a robust, multi-dimensional identity outside the parenting role is, across every measured dimension, a more effective, more connected, and more emotionally available parent than the parent whose identity is primarily or exclusively defined by the role.

This is not a finding about selfishness. It is a finding about a resource. The parent who has their own life — their own passions, their own ambitions, their own relationships that exist independently of the family — is not a parent who cares less about their child. They are parents who have more to bring to the caring. More genuine interest in the child's experience, because they have their own experiences to draw from. More capacity for genuine listening, because they are not listening from a position of desperate need for the connection to go well. More tolerance for the natural distance that a child's growing independence requires, because the distance is not threatening the parent's entire sense of purpose and identity.

The parent who has something of their own, something genuinely theirs, invested in regularly, regarded as non-negotiable, becomes, organically and without effort, the parent their child finds most worth returning to. Not because the child is impressed by the parent's interests. But because the parent who is genuinely alive in their own life is simply more interesting to be around. More present. More capable of the quality of attention that makes a child feel genuinely seen rather than managed. More likely to ask questions out of genuine curiosity than from anxious monitoring. More available, paradoxically, precisely because they are not entirely available. This is the research. And it is the reason the Identity Reclamation Practice is not a peripheral element of the WALLS Framework but one of its five core stages.

16.3 From One Hour to a Full Life

The four weeks of the Identity Reclamation Practice established the foundation. This chapter asks you to build on it — to move from the single investment of one named passion to the broader, more comprehensive vision of who you are in this next chapter. Here is the expanded practice.

The Life Audit

Write, in response to each of the following prompts, for five minutes each without stopping or editing:

Identity beyond parenting: *"Outside my role as a parent, I am someone who ____. The dimensions of my identity that I have most neglected in recent years are ____. The ones I want to invest in deliberately are ____."*

Relationships beyond family: *"The friendships and relationships outside my immediate family that matter most to me are ____. The ones I have allowed to fade that I want to tend to are ____. The quality of connection I want to bring to these relationships is ____."*

Contribution beyond caregiving: *"The ways I want to contribute to the world beyond my family are ____. The skills, experiences, and perspectives I have that are valuable outside* *the parenting role are ____. The contribution I have been deferring that I am ready to begin is ____."*

Ambition beyond the role: *"The ambitions I set aside during the intensive parenting years are ____. The ones that still matter to me — honestly, not performatively — are ____. The one I will begin pursuing, however modestly, is ____."*

These four prompts map the territory of the full identity — the person who exists beyond the parent, who has been present throughout the intensive parenting years, and who is now, for the first time in perhaps a long time, being deliberately and comprehensively invited forward.

Do not filter for practicality. Do not assess the ambitions for likelihood of achievement or the relationships for ease of repair. Write what is true. The practical questions come after the honest inventory, never before it.

The Integration Plan

From the Life Audit, identify the three most energising responses — the three areas where the writing produced the specific flicker of something that felt like genuine, personal desire rather than obligation or aspiration.

For each of the three, write a specific, practical commitment:

What exactly will you do?

How often will you do it?

When will you start, and this answer cannot be "when things settle down," because things will not settle down on a timeline that precedes your investment in this. These three commitments are not resolutions. They are the architecture of the identity you are building, the specific, practical, non-negotiable investments that gradually make the full person real rather than aspirational. Put them in your diary. Protect them with the same seriousness you give to any other commitment you consider important. And when the guilt arrives, as it will, apply the same response you have been learning to apply to every other anxiety-driven voice in this work: name it, check the driver, and choose the hand.

The guilt that says *this time belongs to your child* is the Closed Hand applied to your own life. It deserves the same deliberate, compassionate refusal as every other Closed Hand response this book has been working to change.

16.4 What You Are Modelling

There is a dimension of the Identity Reclamation arc that most parents underestimate — not because they are unaware of the importance of modelling in principle, but because they have not fully considered the specific, powerful thing they model when they deliberately invest in their own lives. They are not modelling selfishness. They are not modelling neglect. They are modelling what it looks like to be a whole person.

The child who observes a parent who is genuinely alive in their own life , who has passions, friendships, and ambitions, and a quality of presence in the world that exists independently of the family, is watching a living demonstration of something that no lecture, no advice, and no managed guidance can produce.

They are watching someone who has chosen, deliberately and at some personal cost, to release fear and invest in trust. To stop organising their identity around what might go wrong and begin organising it around what genuinely matters to them. To model, in the full visibility of daily life, the open-handed approach to their own existence that this book has been asking them to bring to their relationship with their child.

The research on parental modelling of emotional regulation, specifically Siegel's work on interpersonal neurobiology and the intergenerational transmission of attachment patterns, is clear on one point that the Identity Reclamation arc directly addresses: the child who observes a parent managing anxiety through control learns to manage their own anxiety through control. The child who observes a parent managing anxiety through trust, genuine self-investment, and the deliberate cultivation of a life fuller than fear learns something entirely different.

They learn that it is possible to live without the grip. That the open hand is not a naive or fragile response to an uncertain world. That the person who trusts — themselves, their relationships, the world's capacity to hold them — is not less safe than the person who controls. They are freer.

That lesson, modelled daily in the ordinary visible texture of a parent's life, is the most valuable thing this parent can give their child. Not the protected consequence or the managed outcome. The show possibility of a life lived with open hands.

16.5 The Legacy Vision

The Identity Reclamation Practice ends — and this chapter ends — with the **Legacy Vision**: the long-view articulation of how you want to be remembered by your child.

Not in a eulogy. In the ordinary, specific, day-to-day texture of the relationship, as your child will carry it forward into their own adult life. In the quality of memory they will have of what it felt like to be your child — what the relationship taught them about love, about trust, about whether the people who say they believe in you actually do. Here is the practice.

Sit quietly for five minutes; no writing yet. Let the question settle in you without immediately reaching for an answer.

"When my child is fifty years old and thinks about what our relationship taught them about love — what do I want them to know?"

Not what do I want them to think of me? Not what do I want them to say at a funeral? What do I want them to know — in their bones, from the accumulated lived experience of being in relationship with me across the decades of their life?

Then write. For as long as it takes. Without editing for humility or trimming for what seems achievable. Write the full Legacy Vision, the specific, emotionally honest, deeply personal articulation of the parent you are becoming and the love you now offer. It might include:

The way you want them to remember is by being asked questions that were genuinely curious about rather than strategically directed. The way you want them to remember being trusted with their own decisions, even the ones that were difficult to watch. The way you want them to remember the feeling of bringing their real selves into a room with you and finding, instead of management, genuine presence. The way you want them to know, from the experience of being loved by you, that love does not demand to be held, that the open hand holds more than the closed fist ever could. Write it. Keep it alongside the Legacy Letter from Chapter 11. Return to both documents in the tough seasons, not as measures of how far you still have to go, but as the clearest potential evidence of where you are already pointed.

16.6 The Parent You Always Meant to Be

There is a parent who has been waiting inside the intensive, fear-driven, grip-tightened version of parenting that brought you to this book. They are patient. They are not angry about the years it took to arrive here. They understand, with a compassion that the fear never quite allowed, that the pattern that brought you here was built from love — imperfectly expressed, anxiety-driven, inherited from people who were also doing the best they knew how. They have been present throughout, in every moment when the fear was quiet enough that the love could simply be itself.

That parent is not an aspiration. They are not a future version of you that you are working toward from a long way away. They are the version of you that this work has been gradually, consistently, sometimes painfully uncovering, layer by layer, chapter by chapter, one deliberate choice and one open hand at a time.

You have walked through five doorways. You have named the pattern, traced its origins, honoured the grief beneath it, reckoned with its cost, built the map and the compass, and practised the most demanding practical work that the WALLS Framework asks. You have navigated the specific, real-world applications of the framework through the resistant teenager, the adult child, the co-parenting relationship, and the seasons when nothing seemed to work. And you have, across all of it, been becoming someone different. Not a different person. A fuller one.

The parent you always meant to be was never somewhere else. They were here, waiting for the fear to become quiet enough that the love could finally speak first. The fear has not disappeared. But it is no longer the loudest voice in the room. And the parent whose love speaks first, whose first response to their child is curiosity rather than monitoring, trust rather than anxiety, presence rather than management, is the parent their child was always waiting for. You are that parent now. Not perfectly. Not without the ongoing practice that the Consistency Protocol and the daily Three-Second Check and the continuing investment in your own life require. But genuinely. And that genuineness, felt by a child who has been watching, perhaps for longer than you realised, is what changes everything.

The Full Identity Reclamation Arc at a Glance

Practice	What It Requires	What It Produces
The Life Audit	Four prompts, five minutes each, written without filtering for practicality	A complete, honest inventory of the full identity—beyond the parenting role, across relationships, contribution, and ambition
The Integration Plan	Three specific, practical, diary-protected commitments from the Life Audit's most energising responses	The architecture of the full identity—specific enough to be real, practical enough to be sustained
Parental Modelling	The daily, visible investment in a life that is full and genuinely one's own	A living demonstration to the watching child of what it looks like to manage anxiety through trust rather than control
The Legacy Vision	A sustained, unfiltered, emotionally honest articulation of how the parent wants to be remembered by their child	The clearest possible north star for the open-handed parenting journey—specific, personal, and worth every difficult page it took to reach

Table 16: Showing the Full Identity Reclamation Arc at a Glance

Key Takeaway 16

The parents' own transformation is not a detour from the relationship they are trying to build; it is the most direct route to it. The parent who rediscovers who they are outside the intensive parenting role becomes, organically and inevitably, the parent their child finds most worth returning to. You are not yet becoming that parent. You have been becoming them since the moment you chose, on the night you found this book, to begin.

The relationship on the other side of that becoming is not a reward for the work you've done. It is the natural, inevitable expression of a love that has finally been freed from everything that was speaking louder than it.

Chapter 17 addresses what happens when the relationship responds, when the first voluntary contact arrives, when the conversation flows naturally for the first time in what feels like years, when the child brings something real, and the parent receives it with the Open Hand, and something in the room shifts.

Because of this *moment, the moment it* works, *carries its own specific challenge. And the parent who is not prepared for it is the parent most at risk of undoing,* in the breakthrough's relief, *everything the* sustained, arduous work *has built. Chapter 17 is where you learn to hold what you've built — gently, steadily, and with the same open hand that built it.*

Chapter Seventeen

When It's Working — What to Do Next

The moment the relationship responds is one of the least prepared-for moments in this entire journey, and one of the most important to get right. You will recognize it when it arrives. Not necessarily as a dramatic breakthrough, a sudden outpouring of everything that has been withheld across the months of distance. More likely, it will be something quieter than that. A text sent voluntarily, without a prompt. A conversation that runs longer than it has in months, that goes somewhere genuine without being steered. A moment at the dinner table where your child says something real , something that carries the specific quality of a person who has decided, provisionally and without fanfare, to let you in a little further.

That moment is precious. It is also, in a specific and practical sense, fragile. And the parent who has worked with extraordinary care and consistency to create the conditions for it is, paradoxically, the parent most at risk of undermining it in the relief of its arrival.

Because relief, when it finally comes after a long and unrewarded season of open-handed work, has a specific and understandable effect on the parent who has been waiting for it. It relaxes the discipline. It loosens the practice. It produces, gently, invisibly, and with the best of intentions , a subtle return to the patterns that the work has been building away from. Not dramatically. Not all at once. But incrementally, how all deeply conditioned patterns reassert themselves when the pressure that was keeping them at bay has lifted. The child who has been watching closely — the child who has been tentatively and provisionally building a new internal model of what this parent is like now, notices the incremental return. And the door that was opening begins, quietly, to close again.

This chapter is the preparation for that moment. The specific, practical guidance for how to hold what you have built , gently, steadily, and with the same open hand that built it , when the relationship responds, and every instinct says the hard work is done. The hard work is not done. It has simply entered its most rewarding and most sustaining phase.

17.1 Why the Breakthrough Moment Is a Threshold, Not a Destination

The parent who has been waiting for evidence that the framework is working tends to experience the breakthrough moment as a destination when the evidence arrives. As the point they have been working toward finally reached. As permission, in some quiet internal sense, to exhale and ease the discipline that has sustained the work through the unrewarded seasons.

This is entirely understandable. The sustained, patient, consistent effort of open-handed parenting through the hard seasons, through the hostility, the silence, the monosyllables, and the seasons when nothing seemed to work, is genuinely exhausting. A visible response is a genuine milestone. It deserves to be received as such. But it is a threshold, not a destination. The relationship that is responding is not yet the relationship the work is building toward. It is the first evidence that the relationship the work is building toward is possible, and that is a unique thing entirely.

The new relationship is still forming. It is still tender. It is still being assessed, moment by moment, by a child who has learned not to trust that change is real and who, even in the breakthrough moment, watches for the first sign of reversion. Not because they want the change to be false, they want it to be real, with the same fragile hope their parents carry. But because their history with this parent has taught them to treat hope as a hypothesis to be tested rather than a gift to be accepted.

The breakthrough moment is the hypothesis that is being offered. The months of consistent, open-handed parenting that follow it are evidence that the hypothesis is correct. Hold the Open Hand. Not because the relationship is still failing, it is beginning, visibly and measurably, to succeed. But because the success is still fragile, the hand that built it is the hand that will sustain it.

17.2 The Three Risks of the Breakthrough Moment

There are three specific ways in which a parent who has worked hard and well can inadvertently undermine the breakthrough moment. Naming them in advance, before the breakthrough arrives, is what makes them navigable rather than simply painful in retrospect.

Risk 1 — The Overcorrection

The parent who has been holding the Open Hand through a long season of minimal response tends, when the child begins to move toward them, to open too wide. To move from the patient, consistent, agenda-free presence of the Loosen and Listen stages to an intensity of engagement that, however loving its intention, reintroduces the pressure the child was just beginning to relax in response to.

The open question asked once becomes three open questions asked in rapid succession. The genuine conversation that flows naturally becomes a conversation the parent is now steering toward depth, significance, and the emotional intimacy they have been missing. The voluntary text is followed immediately by a response so warm, so comprehensive, and so unmistakably eager that it communicates, beneath the warmth, a quality of need that the child has not forgotten how to read.

The overcorrection is the Closed Hand in the shape of enthusiasm. It is the parent's own unacknowledged grief and longing for closeness — both of which are legitimate, expressing themselves at a volume that is slightly too loud for the fragile new quality of contact the child is tentatively offering.

The antidote is the same three-second check that has governed every significant interaction in this framework. In the breakthrough moment, run it specifically for the overcorrection risk. Name the Hand. Check the Driver. And if the driver is relieved and longing rather than genuinely present and curious, slow down. Receive what is being offered at the pace it is being offered. The relationship will go deeper when it is ready. Your job is to be there when it is, not to pull it there before it is.

Risk 2 — The Premature Relaxation of Practice

The second risk is subtler than the first and, many times, more damaging. It is the gradual, unconscious relaxation of the specific practices that produced the breakthrough, the daily Three-Second Check becoming less consistent, the weekly review skipped because things are going well, the monthly WALLS assessment deferred because the assessment would be positive, and the positive assessment does not feel urgent.

The Consistency Protocol, which Chapter 10 introduced as the bridge between insight and lasting change, is most valuable precisely in the periods when the relationship is going well — because those are the periods when the neural pathway of deliberate choice most needs reinforcement and least receives it.

The parent who maintains their practice through the unrewarded seasons and then relaxes it at the first sign of reward is the parent who discovers, months later, that the relationship has quietly returned to a pattern that is closer to the old one than they realised. Not because the transformation was false; it was real. But because transformation, like any living thing, requires ongoing attention to remain vital.

Maintain the Consistency Protocol through the breakthrough season with the same commitment you brought to it through the difficult one. Not with the same urgency; the urgency belongs to the earlier stages. But with the same regularity, the same honesty, and the same willingness to notice drift before it becomes distance.

Risk 3 — The Unspoken Expectation

The third risk is the most psychologically complex and the most common. It is the emergence, in the parent who has worked hard and consistently and has finally seen results, of an unspoken expectation that is deeply present: *now that the relationship is responding, the child will continue to respond.*

Not a demand. Not an ultimatum. A quiet, internal assumption that the breakthrough marks a new baseline — that the voluntary text will continue to arrive, that the conversations that went somewhere real will become the relationship's new normal, that the child who opened the door a little will continue to open it further at a pace that feels, to the parent, like progress.

That expectation, however natural, however earned by the quality of work that preceded the breakthrough, is the Closed Hand in the shape of hope. And the child who encounters it, who sends one voluntary text and then, for ordinary reasons entirely unrelated to the relationship, does not send another for two weeks, will encounter in the parent's response to that absence of a quality of disappointment that communicates, clearly, that the contact was needed rather than welcomed. The needed contact is not a free contact. The child who understands that their communication is being monitored against an expectation, however unstated, begins, carefully and without drama, to manage their communication accordingly.

Release the expectation. Every contact, however frequent or infrequent, is received as a gift rather than as a fulfillment of a promise. The relationship's pace is the child's to set. The parents' job is to be genuinely, warmly, unhurriedly available at whatever pace the child chooses , and to have enough going on in their own life, built through the Identity Reclamation Practice, that the pace of the child's contact does not determine the quality of the parent's week.

17.3 Deepening the Practice in the Flourishing Season

The Consistency Protocol, in the breakthrough season and the flourishing that follows it, does not simply maintain; it deepens. Here is how each level of the protocol strengthens as the relationship develops. The Daily Five-Minute Check-In: From Discipline to Delight.

In the hard seasons, the daily check-in was a discipline. An act of will applies in the absence of reward. In the flourishing season, it can become something different: a genuine, mutually enjoyed moment of ordinary connection that neither party has to work hard to sustain.

The Open Question practice in this season can expand beyond the five structures of Chapter 10 into a more natural, less structured quality of genuine curiosity, because the relational conditions for genuine exchange have been sufficiently established, so the specific scaffolding of the five structures is no longer always required. The conversation finds its own shape. This is not a signal to abandon the practice. It is a signal that the practice has become part of the relationship's natural texture, which is exactly what the Consistency Protocol was always designed to produce.

The Weekly Twenty-Minute Review: From Assessment to Integration

In the tough seasons, the weekly review was primarily an assessment tool, identifying the moments of most successful Open Hand engagement and the moments of most significant Closed Hand pull, and looking for patterns in the data.

In the flourishing season, it strengthens into something more like integration, a regular, reflective practice in which the parent not only reviews the week's interactions but articulates, with increasing specificity, what the transformation has meant. Not just what changed in the relationship, but what changed in them. How they experience themselves differently as parents. What the open-handed approach has revealed about their own capacity for trust, for genuine presence, for the particular quality of love that does not demand to be held.

This reflection, done regularly across the flourishing season, produces a depth of self-knowledge that continues to inform the quality of the parent's engagement long after the initial transformation work is complete. The Monthly WALLS Assessment: From Recovery to Sustaining.

In the tough seasons, the monthly WALLS assessment was primarily a diagnostic tool, checking position on the map, identifying drift, and returning the parent to the framework's active practice when the demanding conditions of real family life had produced regression.

In the flourishing season, it grows into a sustaining practice, a regular, structured opportunity to assess not just where the parent is within the framework but what the framework has made possible. To document concretely and with specific examples the distance that has been travelled. To notice and name the relationship as it is now, alongside the relationship as it was on the night the parent found this book.

That documentation is not nostalgic. It is motivating because the parent who can see clearly how far the relationship has come is the parent most equipped to sustain the open-handed work through the inevitable difficult moments that real, ongoing family life will continue to produce.

17.4 Sustaining the Open Hand Through Ongoing Challenges

The flourishing season does not mean the end of difficulties. It means the beginning of a unique quality of difficulty, the ongoing, ordinary, adult-terrain challenges of a genuine relationship between two people who love each other and do not always agree. There will still be life choices that are difficult to watch. The career path that concerns you. The relationship partner you have reservations about. The financial decision that you would make differently. The health choice that you cannot make for them, and cannot stop worrying about.

The Open Hand is not indifferent in these situations. It is not the performance of not caring in order to appear more evolved than you feel. It is the genuine, practised, hard-won capacity to hold your concern and your trust simultaneously ,to care deeply about the outcome without requiring your involvement in the path toward it. Here is the specific practice for sustaining the Open Hand through the ongoing challenges of a flourishing relationship:

Name the concern privately before speaking it. Run the Fear Audit on the specific situation, write the concern, the fear beneath it, and the diagnostic question: *If I were not afraid, would I still say this?* If the answer is yes, if the concern is genuine care rather than anxiety, it may belong in the conversation, offered once, as an open question rather than a statement of the problem. If the answer is no, if the concern is fear rather than care, it belongs in the journal, not in the conversation.

Distinguish between invited and uninvited input. The adult child who asks for the parent's perspective on a decision is offering an invitation. The parent who provides their perspective without being asked is operating from the Closed Hand, however genuinely the perspective is held, and however warmly it is delivered. The distinction between these two situations is one of the most important ongoing practices for a flourishing relationship.

Maintain the Evidence File actively. The Evidence File, built through the Loosen stage as a counter to the catastrophising loop, is no less useful in the flourishing season than it was in the difficult one. Every instance in which your child navigates a challenge, the career difficulty managed with more resilience than you expected, the relationship difficulty handled with more wisdom than the anxiety predicted, belongs in the Evidence File. Let it continue to grow. Let it continue to rebalance the anxiety's threat assessment against the reality of the capable, resilient person your child has always been.

17.5 The Pay It Forward Practice

There is a last practice in Chapter 17 that has no equivalent anywhere else in the framework, because it addresses something that the previous chapters were not yet ready to address: what the parent does with what they have learned, now that they have learned it. The **Pay It Forward Practice** is the choice to make the hard-won experience of this transformation available to another parent who is at the beginning of it.

Not by prescribing. Not by positioning yourself as someone who has arrived at a place others have not yet reached. By being honest, when the context is right, and the opportunity presents itself, about the journey you have taken, what it has cost, and what it has produced.

The parent who tells another parent, at the school gate, at the family gathering, in the late-night text exchange with a friend who says *I don't know what's happening with my daughter, nothing I do is working*, that they have been in that place, and that they found a way through it, and that the way through it is not what the fear is currently telling them it is: that parent has done something that is simultaneously generous to the other parent and consolidating to themselves.

Generous, because the parent who is currently in the unrewarded season of open-handed work needs, more than almost anything, the testimony of someone who has been there and come through. Not advice, testimony. The honest, specific, personal account of what the work felt like from the inside and what it produced. Consolidating, because the parent who articulates their own transformation to another person in the middle of that person's struggle does something that private reflection alone cannot fully achieve: they make the transformation irrevocably their own. The parent who teaches open-handed love to another parent has made it, in the deepest possible sense, part of who they are. The Pay It Forward Practice is not an obligation. It is an invitation, and the parent who accepts it will discover that the generosity it asks for is also, unexpectedly, one of the most powerful consolidations of everything this book has built.

The Flourishing Season Practices at a Glance

Practice	What It Requires	What It Produces
Holding the breakthrough moment	Recognising and navigating the three risks — overcorrection, premature relaxation, and unspoken expectation	The fragile new quality of contact was sustained and deepened rather than inadvertently closed again
Deepening the Consistency Protocol	Evolving the daily, weekly, and monthly practices from discipline to delight, assessment to integration, recovery to sustaining	A living practice that continues to inform and strengthen the relationship long after the initial transformation is complete
Sustaining the Open Hand through ongoing challenges	The private Fear Audit, before spoken concern, the invited-versus-uninvited distinction, and the continued active Evidence File	The open-handed relationship sustained through the inevitable ongoing difficulties of real family life
The Pay It Forward Practice	Honest testimony, offered when the context is right, to another parent at the beginning of this journey	The transformation made irrevocably one's own, and a contribution that multiplies the work's reach into relationships the parent will never directly touch

Table 17: Showing the Flourishing Season Practices at a Glance

Key Takeaway 17

Flourishing is not a state that requires no maintenance; **it is a living relationship that deepens with every open-handed choice made after the initial transformation.** The parent who reaches this stage and sustains it through the ongoing challenges of real family life has not just repaired a relationship. They have built a new one, and the love that built it will last.

Not because it is perfect. Not because the difficult moments are behind them. But because the parent who has come this far has developed something that no difficult moment can permanently undo: the genuine, practised, hard-won capacity to choose the Open Hand.

That capacity is not borrowed. It is not contingent on good conditions, cooperative children, or favourable circumstances. It is theirs. Built through every deliberate choice, every logged interaction, every stayed Three-Second Check, and every held silence and every released outcome across the weeks and chapters of this work. It is theirs. And it will last.

Chapter 18 is the final chapter, and it is the one this entire book has been building toward. Not the destination of the journey, but the full, vivid, emotionally specific vision of the relationship that open-handed love creates, painted not as an aspiration but as a credible, earned, entirely attainable reality. And the completion of the Legacy Letter. And the single most important truth the book has been holding for you since the Introduction. It is time to receive it.

Chapter Eighteen

The Relationship You Were Always Building Toward

This is the chapter that was always waiting at the end of the work. Not as a reward for completing it. Not as a destination that the journey has finally deposited you at after all the difficulty and the discipline and the unrewarded seasons of open-handed effort. But as the honest, credible, entirely attainable articulation of what the love you have been building, one deliberate choice, one released outcome, one Open Hand at a time, can produce.

You opened this book on a tough night. The house was quiet. Something had happened, or something hadn't happened that you needed to happen, and the particular combination of love and fear and exhaustion and grief that brought you to these pages was, in that moment, the most honest thing about you.

That parent, the one who was walking on eggshells, who was loving completely and trying relentlessly and watching in quiet devastation as the relationship strained under the weight of a fear that had been speaking louder than the love for years , that parent is not gone. They are still you. But they are no longer the loudest voice in the room. Something else is louder now. Something that was always present and always real and always the truest thing about the relationship you have been so afraid of losing. The love. Not the fear-driven version, not the love that grips and monitors and pre-empts and intervenes. The love that trusts. The love that is genuinely curious about who this person is becoming. The love that can sit in the same room as difficulty and uncertainty, and the natural distance of a child growing more fully into themselves, and hold the Open Hand steady. That love is what this chapter is about. And the relationship it creates, painted here in this final chapter, not as aspiration but as reality, is the relationship you were always building toward.

18.1 The Relationship on the Other Side

Let yourself receive this. Not as something you are still working toward from a long distance. As something that is already, in the accumulated quality of every open-handed choice you have made since Chapter 1, beginning to take shape. The relationship on the other side of open-handed love is not a repaired version of what existed before. It is not the restoration of the closeness of the early years; that season is gone, and its passing deserves the honest grief that Chapter 3 gave it. It is not the return of the family as it once was, gathered around the table in the particular texture of a Saturday morning that belonged to an earlier chapter.

It is something new. Something that neither parent nor child could have built while the grip was still in place, because the grip prevented the very conditions under which this relationship could grow. The conditions it needed were not perfect behaviour, an absence of difficulty, or a child who cooperated with the parent's attempts to change. The conditions it needed were exactly what the WALLS Framework has been building, stage by stage and choice by choice, across the chapters of this book.

A parent who could see clearly without being destroyed by what they saw. A parent who could own the cost honestly without being paralysed by the shame of it. A parent who could loosen the grip even when every conditioned response was screaming to tighten it. A parent who could listen without an agenda and wait without an expectation, and be present without a need for the presence to be received in a particular way.

And a parent whose own life was full enough, whose identity was whole enough, whose sense of self was sufficiently distributed across enough dimensions of meaning and contribution and genuine personal investment, that the relationship with their child could be the richest thread in a rich fabric rather than the only thread in an empty one.

That parent is one who you have been becoming. And the relationship available to that parent is something that the fear, in all its persuasive certainty about what was and was not possible, never allowed you to fully imagine. Let yourself imagine it now.

18.2 The Voluntary Phone Call

It arrived on an ordinary Tuesday. Not a birthday, not a holiday, not the occasion that produces obligatory contact regardless of the underlying quality of the relationship. An ordinary Tuesday, and the phone rings, and it is your child, and they are calling not because they should but because something happened, and you are the person they wanted to tell.

That call does not feel like the product of a framework, a practice, or the accumulated months of deliberate, unrewarded, open-handed work. It feels like your child is calling because they wanted to. Because the relationship has become, quietly and without fanfare, the relationship people turn to when something matters.

It is a slight moment. It is also one of the specific, emotionally precise images you named in your Flourish Markers, the one that, in the tough seasons when the progress was invisible, you returned to as the face of the destination. And now it is not an image. It is Tuesday.

Receive it the way the Open Hand receives things: without gripping it, without immediately needing it to mean more than it means, without the relief and the longing and the months of patient waiting expressing themselves at a volume that is slightly too loud for the moment.

Just received it. Be genuinely glad. Be genuinely curious about what they are calling to tell you. Ask the Open Question and listen without preparing. Let the conversation be what it is, in its ordinary, unforced, freely chosen quality, the most extraordinary thing that the work of this book has produced.

18.3 The Sunday Dinner Chosen Freely

There will be a Sunday when the invitation to dinner is extended and accepted, not from obligation, not from the particular guilt that can produce attendance without presence, but because your home is a place your child actually wants to be. They arrive in their own time, carrying the ordinary details of their own lives: the job, the relationship, the plans, the preoccupations that constitute the specific texture of the person they are becoming. And they bring these things into the room with you, not because you have asked the right questions, deployed the right framework, or created the right conditions through careful strategic management.

They bring them because the room is safe. Because the person waiting in it has proven, through the quality of every interaction since this book began, that what arrives in this room will be received, not managed. That which is shared will be heard, not redirected. That the relationship between parent and child, in this room, on this Sunday, has become something neither the parent's fear nor the child's protective distance could have built: a relationship of genuine mutual choosing.

You did not manufacture this Sunday. You built the conditions for it, one open-handed choice at a time, across the weeks and months and hard seasons of a transformation that cost you something real and produced something more valuable than anything the grip was trying to protect.

18.4 The Conversation That Goes Somewhere Real

It will not always be about something significant. The conversation that goes somewhere real, in the relationship that open-handed love creates, is often about something entirely ordinary: a film, a memory, a passing observation about something neither of you had thought about in years.

But it will have a quality to it that the managed conversations of the Closed Hand years never had. A quality of genuine exchange — of two people who are actually present with each other, actually curious about each other's experience, actually interested in where the conversation goes rather than where the anxiety or the grief or the pattern of management would have steered it.

That quality is not a technique. It is not the product of the Open Question practice being deployed correctly or of the Three-Hand Method being applied with sufficient consistency. It is the natural expression of a relationship that has, at last, the conditions for genuine connection, because the parent in it is no longer parenting from fear.

The conversation goes somewhere real because the parent is somewhere real. Present. Genuinely interested. Not managing the destination. Just there, with the full quality of attention that the open-handed approach, practised across the stages of this work, has made available.

That quality of presence is a gift. Everything the conversation produces— the laughter, the honesty, the moments of genuine recognition between two people who share a history and are still, always, discovering each other— is the relationship it was always possible to have. The relationship that neither of you could build while the grip was still in place.

18.5 The Moment of Genuine Adult Friendship

There is a moment, it arrives differently for every parent, in the specific, unscripted, particular way that all the most important moments arrive, when the relationship stops feeling like a parent-child relationship and begins feeling like something else as well. Not instead of. As well as.

The parent-child bond does not disappear. The love that has been present since the child's first breath does not transform into something unrecognisable. But alongside it, quietly and without announcement, something new has grown: the specific, particular, mutually chosen quality of genuine adult friendship between two people who happen also to be parent and child.

It is not something the parent can manufacture. It cannot be produced by applying the right framework at the right moment or by the sustained consistency of the right practices over the right number of weeks. It grows organically in the conditions that the open-handed work creates, and when it arrives; it arrives as recognition rather than achievement.

Recognition that this person, this specific, particular, fully formed human being who shares your history and carries your eyes and has been, through all the years of fear and grief and distance and work, becoming more fully themselves, is someone you would choose. Not just as a child you love, but as a person you genuinely, freely, with clear eyes and an open hand, choose to have in your life.

And the recognition that they are choosing you back. Not from obligation, not from the complicated loyalty of the family bond, not from the managed compliance of a relationship built on the Closed Hand's expectations. From genuine affection. From the real, specific, chosen quality of a connection that has been built slowly, honestly, at considerable cost to both of you, on the most durable foundation available. Trust.

18.6 Completing the Legacy Letter

This is the moment to return to the Legacy Letter you began in Chapter 11. The private, unsealed letter to your child that was never intended to be sent, only to be kept, as the clearest potential evidence of where you are and who you have become and what the love you are offering now actually looks like.

Read what you wrote there. Read it with the full knowledge of what has happened since the stages walked through, the practices sustained, the hard seasons navigated, the breakthrough moments received and held with an open hand. Read it as the document of a parent who was already, in the moment of writing it, becoming the person who every chapter since has been continuing to build.

And then add to it. One last section, the section that could only be written here, from the other side of the work, with the relationship that open-handed love creates already beginning to take the shape you named in your Flourish Markers.

Write it to your child. In your own voice. From everything you now know about what this work has cost and what it has produced and what the love you are offering, with open hands, with clear eyes, with the specific courage it took to get here, can create.

You do not need a template for this section. You have everything you need. You have spent this entire book building the language, honesty, and self-knowledge that this final section requires.

Write it.

And then close the letter. Set it somewhere safe. Not as an archive, but as a living document. Return to it in the difficult seasons, in the moments of doubt, in the days when the old pattern stirs, and the Three-Second Check stands between the relationship as it is and the relationship as it was.

Return to it and remember who you are now. Not who you were when you opened this book. Who you are now: the parent whose love speaks first, whose hand is open, whose child is not held but chosen.

18.7 The Truth This Book Has Been Building Toward

Since the Introduction, since the very first page, before the first framework had been introduced, before the first practice had been named, this book has been carrying a single truth toward this moment.

Not saving it. Carrying it. Planting it in the Introduction so the reader would carry it into every chapter, returning to it again and again in the moments when the work was hard, and the reward was invisible, and the fear was louder than the love. Here it is, delivered now in its fullest and most personal form. **The open hand holds more**

than the clenched fist ever could. Not as a metaphor. As the specific, lived, hard-won reality of a parent who has done this work, who has released the grip that felt like love, who has chosen trust over the anxiety that was masquerading as care, who has held the Open Hand through the hostility and the silence and the unrewarded seasons and the fragile breakthrough moments and the ongoing ordinary challenges of a real relationship between two people who love each other.You have proven this. Not in theory. In the specific, particular, irreplaceable texture of your own relationship with your own child, built from the specific, particular, irreplaceable work you have done across the chapters of this book.

The grip would never give you the relationship you wanted. It was always going to give you exactly what it produced: a child who moved toward the door, not because they stopped loving you, but because the love being offered required them to choose between closeness and becoming themselves.

The Open Hand gives them both. The closeness and the becoming. The relationship and the self. The parent who trusts and the child who, eventually, on their own terms, in their own time, in the particular, unforced, freely chosen way that all the most valuable things arrive, chooses to come home.

18.8 The Parent Their Child Is Waiting For

The parent whose child is waiting for is not a different person. They are not someone with better instincts, fewer fears, or a childhood that produced a healthier emotional toolkit. They are not someone who has never operated from the Closed Hand, never sent the follow-up text, never rewritten the essay, or never felt the particular, overwhelming quality of love-as-anxiety that has been the subject of this entire book.

They are the same person who found this book on a hard night. The same person who has loved their child with the full force of everything they are, from their first breath until right now. The same person whose fear has been louder than their love for longer than they would have chosen, and who chose, across the chapters behind you, to change that.

That is who the child is waiting for. That parent, this parent, is finally free from the fear that has been speaking louder than their love for years.

The relationship you were always building toward is not in the future. It is not contingent on more work or better conditions, or a child who finally cooperates, or a season when things are easier. It is here. Built imperfectly and honestly and with extraordinary courage, from what can be, from exactly where you are, from exactly who you have become. The love that lasts in any relationship is always the love that does not demand to be held. You know this now. Not as a sentence on a page, but as the lived, embodied, hard-won truth of a parent who opened their hands and discovered that what they were holding, the relationship that both parties were always capable of was more than anything the grip was ever trying to protect.

Hold it gently. Keep choosing it. And know that the love you are offering now, with open hands, with clear eyes, with the particular courage it took to get here, is the love that will last.

Key Takeaway 18

The relationship on the other side of open-handed love is not a repaired version of what existed before. It is something neither parent nor child could have built while the grip was still in place, a relationship of genuine mutual choosing, freely given closeness, and the particular joy of an adult friendship that was always possible and is now, at last, real. You did not fix a broken relationship. You built a new one on the most durable foundation available. And the love that built it will last.

The Conclusion follows in Chapter 19 — the full, last celebration of the distance you have travelled, the transformation you have lived, and the parent you have become. And then, in the Appendices, the complete toolkit: every practice, every framework, every tool this book has offered, assembled in one place for the moments when you need to return to the map, reset the compass, and remember exactly where you are.

You are nearly at the end of the book. You are nowhere near the end of the work, because the work now *is simply being the parent you have become. One open-handed day at a time. That is not a burden. It is the life you were always building toward.*

Chapter Nineteen

Conclusion: The Open Hand Is the Strongest Hold

You started this book on an arduous night. You were sitting somewhere quiet; the house settled around you, the events of the evening still vibrating somewhere in your chest, and you were holding, in some form, the particular combination of love and fear and exhaustion that has been the subject of every page since. You were uncertain that anything could change. You may not have been certain you deserved for anything to change. But you were here. And the fact that you were here, that you chose on that night to reach toward something different rather than simply carrying what you were carrying back to bed, is not a small thing. It is, in fact, the thing. The first deliberate choice of an open-handed parent in the making. Look how far that choice has brought you.

19.1 The Distance You Have Travelled

You have walked through five doorways. Each one demanded something real of you, not the comfortable, aspirational version of change, but the specific, practised, sometimes deeply uncomfortable work of a person who looked honestly at their own pattern and chose, one moment at a time, to build something different.

You Witnessed. You conducted the Fear Audit with the specificity that made it workable rather than merely honest. You named the grief that had been operating underground, the loss of being needed completely, the loss of the earlier season, the loss of the version of yourself you were in those years, and gave it language for the first time. You built the map upon which every stage of this work has been built: clear, compassionate, honest, and specific enough to actually change something.

You Acknowledged. You wrote the Cost Inventory and looked at what your pattern had cost, on your child, on the relationship, on yourself, without softening the numbers or retreating into the shame that would have made the looking unbearable. You converted regret into agency. You made the irrevocable internal decision that was not a hope or an intention but a commitment: something is going to change.

You Loosened. You deployed the Three-Hand Method as your daily operating system and built the neural pathway of deliberate choice through the most practically demanding stage of the entire framework. You executed the Deliberate Step Back, in a real situation, with a real consequence allowed to land, and discovered, in your own Evidence File, the first personal, irrefutable record that your child is more capable than your anxiety has been telling you they are. You survived the discomfort. Every time. And every time the pathway grew stronger.

You Listened. You mastered the Open Question practice and developed the discipline of listening without preparing. You initiated the Repair Conversation three sentences, released completely, offered as a gift rather than a transaction. You implemented the Consistency Protocol and converted the book's insights from a reading experience into a daily, weekly, and monthly living practice. You built the bridge, plank by plank, across the distance that fear had created.

You Soared. You invested in the Identity Reclamation Practice and began the serious, non-negotiable work of reclaiming the person who exists beyond the parenting role. You defined your Flourish Markers, the specific, emotionally precise images of the relationship as it will be when the open-handed love you are building has had the time and consistency it needs. You wrote the Legacy Letter. And you stepped deliberately and with full eyes open into the life you were always building toward.

That is not a small journey. That is the journey that most parents who love their children as much as you do never take, not because they lack the love, but because nobody ever gave them the map, the compass, or the permission to see the pattern clearly enough to change it. You had all three. And you walked.

19.2 The WALLS You Have Moved Through

The WALLS Framework was not designed to eliminate the walls between parent and child. It showed the parent that the walls were always doorways, that every stage of the distance growing between them was a stage of a child becoming more fully themselves, requiring from the parent not a tighter grip but a more open hand. You entered the framework carrying the walls. You are leaving it, carrying the doorways.

Witness gave you an honest, compassionate, shame-free view of exactly where you were. Not a verdict, but a starting point. And from that starting point, everything became possible that had previously seemed impossible, because the thing you can see clearly, you can work with. The thing you cannot see, or can only see through the distorting lens of shame, drives you.

Acknowledge gave you the fuel. Not the fuel of guilt that paralyzes, but the fuel of guilt that points forward, the specific, felt, fully owned recognition that something real has been happening, at actual cost, to a real person you love. And the irrevocable decision, made from the honest weight of that recognition, that it ends here.

Loosen gave you the evidence. Not borrowed evidence, not the research or the theory or the framework's promise, but your own, personal, specific, irrefutable record of a child who is capable, resilient, and more equipped to handle their own life than the anxiety was ever willing to let you believe. That evidence lives in the Evidence File you have been building since Chapter 9. It belongs to you. And it will continue to grow for as long as you keep looking at what is actually in front of you rather than what fear predicts.

Listen gave you the bridge. The five Open Question structures and the discipline of asking without managing. The Repair Conversation and the three sentences that did what a thousand managed interactions could not do: communicated to your child, without agenda and without expectation, that something had genuinely changed. The Consistency Protocol and the daily, weekly, and monthly practice converted that change from a temporary change into a living commitment.

Soar gave you yourself back. The identity that existed before the fear got loud. The life that is yours, full enough, specific enough, genuinely enough invested in, so that the relationship with your child is the richest thread in a rich fabric rather than the only thread in an empty one. The Legacy Letter and the Legacy Vision and the particular, irreplaceable knowledge that the parent you are becoming is not a project you are managing. It is a person you already are.

19.3 The Future You Are Living Into

Paint this with me for a moment. Not as fantasy as the credible, earned, entirely attainable future of a parent who has done what you have done. The voluntary phone call on an ordinary Tuesday. The Sunday dinner chosen freely. The conversation that goes somewhere real because the person you are in it is genuinely present rather than strategically engaged. The moment of adult friendship with the grown child who carries your eyes and your history and is, more and more clearly, someone you would choose even if the bond had not been there from the beginning.

A home that feels different. Not because the difficult moments are gone, they are not, but because the quality of the parent navigating them has changed. Because the first response to difficulty is no longer the Closed Hand reaching to manage, pre-empt, and protect. Because the Three-Second Check has become, through a thousand repetitions, a reflex rather than a discipline. Because love speaks first now.

A version of yourself that you recognize. Not the version that was running on anxiety and exhaustion, and the particular depletion of parenting two lives simultaneously. The version that has reclaimed the identity, the interests, the relationships, and the ambitions that belong to the full person, the one who is also, and always, the parent. The one who models, in the visible texture of daily life, what it looks like to live without the grip.

A legacy. Not the legacy of the parent who held on the hardest. The legacy of the parent who trusted their child enough to let them become exactly who they were always meant to be, and who loved them in a way that left them free. This is not somewhere you are going. It is somewhere you already are in the accumulated quality of every deliberate choice you have made since the night you opened this book, *love with open hands*.

19.4 What You Now Know About Love

There are things you know now that you did not know when you started. Not information, the information was always available. Things that you know in how only lived experience produces knowing: in the body, in the history of a thousand small deliberate choices, in the particular quality of understanding that cannot be borrowed from a book but can, perhaps, be catalysed by one.

You know that anxiety disguised as love is not experienced as love by the person receiving it. Not because the love is false, the love is real and enormous, but because the fear that the love is filtered changes the shape of it into something the child experiences as pressure rather than presence, management rather than connection.

You know that the grief of a child growing up is real, significant, and entirely legitimate, and that the parent who names it honestly stops needing to express it as control.

You know the difference between guilt and shame, not as a theoretical distinction but as a felt, practical one that you have navigated in real time across the chapters of this book. Guilt points forward. Shame collapses inward. You know which one to follow.

You know that the neural pathway of deliberate choice is built through repetition, not revelation. The Three-Second Check is not a technique you deploy in the dramatic moments but a reflex you build in the ordinary ones. That the Open Hand becomes natural, genuinely natural, rather than effortfully performed, only through the accumulation of a thousand small, logged, deliberate choices that gradually replace the default.

You know that consistency in the absence of visible reward is the most powerful signal available to a child who has learned not to trust that change is real. That the unrewarded seasons are not evidence of failure. They are the proof, assembled in the watching child's private assessment, that this time is different.

And you know, in the deepest, most personal, most hard-won sense of knowing, that the love that lasts in any relationship is always the love that does not demand to be held.

19.5 The Open Hand Is the Strongest Hold

There is a paradox at the centre of everything this book has offered. It is the paradox that the fear that drove the grip could never resolve, because the fear's logic is precisely the logic that the paradox dismantles.

The fear said: if I let go, I will lose them.

The truth is that the grip was losing them. And the open hand, the trusting, present, agenda-free, outcome-released, genuinely curious open hand, is what holds them more completely than the grip ever could. Not by keeping them close. By making closeness something they choose. Not by being indispensable. By being worth returning to. Not by managing the relationship into the shape that the fear required. By creating the conditions, through open-handed love, sustained through the tough seasons, offered without demand, held without gripping , under which the relationship could become whatever both parties could always make it.

The open hand is the strongest hold because it does not hold at all. It simply remains open, steady, warm, present, and unhurried, and trusts that what belongs in it will return. Your child belongs in it. Not because you have made it impossible for yourself to leave. Because you have made yourself genuinely worth choosing. That is the transformation. That is what every chapter of this book was building toward. That is what the fear, for all its conviction and all its volume, could never produce on its own. And that is what you have built.

19.6 One Last Thing

The parent whose child is waiting for is not in the future. They are here. They are you, the same person who has loved this child from their first breath, who has tried with everything they had, who found this book on a difficult night and chose, against the full weight of the fear and the grief and the exhaustion, to do something genuinely different.

The relationship you have been imagining, the voluntary phone call, the Sunday dinner chosen freely, the conversation that goes somewhere real, the adult friendship that was always possible and is now, at last, being built, is not contingent on anything you have not already done.

It is contingent only on continuing. On returning to the Consistency Protocol when the tough seasons arrive, as they will. On running the Three-Second Check in the ordinary moments when nobody is watching, and the choice is entirely yours. On maintaining the Open Hand, not because the reward is always visible but because the love that sustains it is real, and enormous, and no longer speaking from behind the fear. You have proven that now. And the love you are offering, with open hands, with clear eyes, with the courage it took to get here, is the love that will last

The Appendices that follow contain the complete Love Without Walls Toolkit: every practice, every framework, every tool this book has offered, assembled in one portable reference. Return to them whenever you need to reset the compass, return to the map, or simply remember what each practice requires and what it produces. The work continues. And the work now is simply being the parent you have become.

One open-handed day at a time.

Chapter Twenty

Appendices

Appendix A: The Love Without Walls Toolkit

*E*very practice and tool from this book is compiled into a single, *portable reference.* Return here whenever you need to reset the compass, locate yourself on the map, or remind yourself what a specific practice requires and what it produces.

Tool 1 — The Fear Audit

What it is: A written self-assessment that maps your most frequent parenting interventions to the specific fears beneath them, distinguishing genuine care from unresolved anxiety.

When to use it: At the beginning of the Witness stage, and whenever you notice the Closed Hand operating with unusual frequency or intensity, as a reset and recalibration tool.

The four steps:

List your ten most frequent interventions from the last two weeks. Write the actual behaviour, in its actual context, not a category, a specific instance.

Name the fear beneath each one. Not a general worry, but the specific, honest fear that was operating in that moment.

Apply the Three-Hand classification. For each behaviour, identify whether it originates from the Closed Hand (fear-driven), the Open Hand (trust-driven), or the Guiding Hand (invited mentorship).

Apply the diagnostic question to each Closed Hand behaviour: *"If I were not afraid right now, would I still do this?"* If the answer is no, this is the behaviour you are working on.

The grief layer addition: For each Closed Hand behaviour, ask a second question: *"Is there a loss underneath this behaviour, something I mourn that this intervention is trying, unconsciously, to hold on to?"* Write one sentence naming the grief, if present.

Tool 2 — The Wall Origin Story

What it is: A guided narrative writing exercise that traces the roots of your anxiety back to your earliest experiences of love, loss, and the grip that followed , giving the pattern a history that makes it understandable rather than shameful.

When to use it: In the Witness stage, after completing the Fear Audit. Allow forty-five minutes in private.

The three parts:

Part 1 — The Family Blueprint (15 minutes) *"In the family I grew up in, love looked like____. Letting go looked like____. When I showed independence, the response was____. The belief I absorbed about what it means to keep someone safe was____."*

Part 2 — The Moment the Grip Formed (15 minutes) *"The first time I understood that love and holding on were the same thing was____. The experience that taught me that letting go was the same as losing was____. After that, the way I loved people changed in the following way:____."*

Part 3 — The Connection to Now (15 minutes) *"I can see this same pattern operating in my parenting in the following specific ways: ____. The fear underneath it connects back to* my history *in this way: ____. Understanding where it came from changes the way I see it, because ____."*

Tool 3 — The Grief Naming Practice

What it is: A structured writing exercise that identifies and articulates each specific loss the current parenting season has brought — because grief that is named can be moved through, and grief that is buried drives behaviour.

When to use it: In the Witness stage, alongside the Fear Audit. Allow thirty minutes in private.

The three parts:

Part 1 — The Inventory of Losses (15 minutes) Write every specific thing you have lost in this season of parenting. Not categories — specific things. The Saturday mornings. The first phone call. The physical closeness. The particular season of family life that has ended.

Part 2 — The Acknowledgement (10 minutes) For each loss on your list, write a single sentence: *"The loss of ____ is real, and it deserves to be mourned."* No reframe. No silver lining. Simply an acknowledgement.

Part 3 — The Separation (5 minutes) For each loss, write: *"This unacknowledged loss has been showing up in my parenting as ____."* This is where the connection between grief and controlling behaviour becomes explicit and workable.

Tool 4 — The Cost Inventory

What it is: A private, structured written document that honestly records the specific relational costs of fear-driven parenting across four dimensions — not as self-punishment, but as the foundation from which genuine, lasting change is built.

When to use it: In the Acknowledge stage. Write it with full specificity, using your child's name and concrete examples rather than general observations.

The four dimensions:

Dimension 1 — The cost to your child's capability. Messages received. Independence undermined. Confidence quietly eroded. The specific ways the pattern has shaped your child's developing sense of their own competence.

Dimension 2 — The cost to the relationship. The conversations that closed. The trust that eroded. The version of your child you don't fully know because the conditions for genuine openness were never built. The withdrawals made from the relational account.

Dimension 3 — The cost to yourself. The identity subsumed by the role. The physiological toll of sustained anxiety. The impact on your partnership or marriage. The ambitions, interests, and dimensions of self quietly set aside.

Dimension 4 — The forward-facing declaration. Write, in your own words, the irrevocable internal decision that the inventory has produced. Not a sentence completion — a personal statement of committed, agentic change. This is the Acknowledge stage, complete.

Tool 5 — The Three-Hand Method

What it is: The real-time diagnostic compass of the Love Without Walls System, a three-second check that makes deliberate choice available in any parenting interaction, however fast and however charged.

When to use it: Every significant parenting interaction. Not occasionally, every time.

The Three Hands:

The Closed Hand: The mode of fear-driven parenting. Monitors, manages, controls, and intervenes. Driven by anxiety rather than genuine care.

The Open Hand: The mode of trust. Allows, waits, asks genuine questions, and listens without redirecting. Tolerates uncertainty because it trusts the child's capabilities.

The Guiding Hand: The mode of mentorship. Invited, boundaried, appropriately present. Offers perspective when asked, wisdom without insisting it be followed.

The Three-Second Check:

Name the Hand. Which hand am I reaching for right now?

Check the Driver. What is driving that reach — fear or genuine care?

Choose the Hand. Is this the hand this moment calls for? If not, which one does?

The Hostile Teenager Addition — Check the Need: *"Am I reaching for the Open Hand because it is genuinely the right response — or because I need this interaction to go well?"* If the driver is need, rather than genuine presence, step back before proceeding.

The daily log (five fields, thirty seconds): Interaction / Hand reached for / Hand chosen / Gap (yes/no) / Condition if gap present

Tool 6 — The Deliberate Step Back

What it is: The centrepiece practice of the Loosen stage, the conscious, structured choice not to intervene in a specific, identified situation, allowing the natural consequence to land in full.

When to use it: In the Loosen stage, beginning with the lowest-anxiety item on your Fear Audit and progressing toward higher-anxiety situations as the neural pathway of deliberate choice strengthens.

The five-step sequence:

Notice the impulse. Feel the familiar reach for the Closed Hand. Name it internally: *This is the impulse. It is not an instruction.*

Run the Three-Second Check. Name the Hand, check the driver, choose the Open Hand.

Do not intervene. Allow the situation to unfold without your management.

Stay present without rescuing. Be physically present and emotionally available without stepping in.

Observe what actually happens. Not what you feared. What actually happens?

The Three-Question Reflection (complete the same evening):

"What did I fear would happen?"

"What actually happened?"

"What does the gap between those two answers tell me?"

Tool 7 — The Evidence File

What it is: A running written record of every instance in which your child handled a difficult situation without parental intervention and showed capability, resilience, or growth, the personal, irrefutable counter-argument to the catastrophising loop.

When to use it: Begin in the Loosen stage. Add an entry after every Deliberate Step Back and every observed instance of your child's capability, in any context. Return to it in any season when the anxiety is loudest and the old pattern is most compelling.

The entry format: Date / Brief description / What your child showed.

Example: 15th March — She had the difficult conversation with her teacher herself, without me contacting the school. It went better than I expected, and she seemed genuinely proud of how she handled it.

The purpose: Not to prove that nothing ever goes wrong. To show, in your own handwriting, from your own life, with your own child, that your anxiety's threat assessment has been consistently and sometimes dramatically overestimating risk and underestimating capability.

Tool 8 — The Open Question Practice

What it is: Five specific question structures that consistently invite a genuine response from a teenager or young adult without triggering defensiveness or the sense of being managed.

When to use it: Daily, in every significant parent-child interaction. Practised with the discipline of listening without preparing — no redirecting, no filling the silence, no composing the response before the answer has been fully given.

The five structures:

Open Question Structures at a Glance

Structure	Examples
Pure Curiosity	"What was the best part of today?" / "What's been on your mind lately?"
Experience	"What was that like for you?" / "How did that feel in the moment?"
Perspective	"What do you think you'll do?" / "What's your instinct on this?"
Reflection	"Looking back, what would you do differently?" / "What did you learn from how that went?"
Future	"What would make that easier next time?" / "What would help?"

Appendix A Table 1: Showing the Five Open Question structures at a Glance

Hostile teenager adaptations:

Radically lower the stakes of the question

Remove the expectation of a response — ask in passing, not as the centrepiece of a connection attempt

Prioritise presence over connection — simply being in the room without an agenda before any question is asked

The listening discipline log: *"I listened without preparing: [yes/partially/no]. The moment I started preparing was ____."*

Tool 9 — The Repair Conversation

What it is: A structured, three-element framework for opening one honest, vulnerable, agenda-free conversation about the relationship — offered as a gift, not a transaction, with the outcome released completely.

When to use it: In the Listen stage, after the Loosen stage has established sufficient behavioural evidence that the change is real. Choose a private, unhurried, low-stakes moment. For teenagers, a car journey is often the most accessible setting.

The three elements:

"I see what has been happening between us." Acknowledgement — stated simply, without elaboration, minimisation, or defensive qualification.

"I am working on changing my part in it." Ownership — present continuous tense, deliberate. Not *I have changed,* or *I will try.* Active, ongoing, evidenced by the behaviour that has already changed.

"I am not asking you to respond; I am showing you something different." Release — the most important and most difficult element. Do not qualify it. Do not, in the days that follow, refer to the conversation or ask whether it was received.

Adult child adaptation: Add the acknowledgement of duration to Element 1: *"I see what has been happening between us — and I see that it has been happening for longer than I have been willing to honestly acknowledge."*

After delivery, say nothing more. Release the outcome completely. Let the conversation do its work in the private space where it will actually be processed.

Tool 10 — The Consistency Protocol

What it is: The daily, weekly, and monthly practice structure that converts the book's insights from a reading experience into a living commitment, the bridge between knowing and lasting change.

When to use it: From the Listen stage onward, maintained through every season, the rewarding ones and the difficult ones equally.

The three levels:

Daily — The Five-Minute Check-In: One genuine, Open Question-structured interaction per day. Ask with genuine curiosity. Listen without preparing. Log one line.

Weekly — The Twenty-Minute Review: Review the daily log. Identify the two moments of most successful Open Hand engagement and the two moments of most significant Closed Hand pull. Write one sentence about what the difficult moments had in common. This is pattern recognition — the level above the individual entry where the larger shape of progress becomes visible.

Monthly — The Sixty-Minute WALLS Assessment Return to the full WALLS Framework. Assess honestly where you are in each stage. Not where you hoped to be — where you are. Identify any drift and name the one specific practice that will return you to the map.

The flourishing season's **evolution:**

Daily check-in: from discipline to delight — the conversation finds its own shape

Weekly review: from assessment to integration — what the transformation has meant, not just what changed

Monthly assessment: from recovery to sustaining — documenting the distance travelled, not just the current position

The Complete Toolkit at a Glance

Tool	Stage	Primary Purpose
1. The Fear Audit	Witness	Map the pattern — behaviours, fears, grief layer
2. The Wall Origin Story	Witness	Trace the pattern's generational origins
3. The Grief Naming Practice	Witness	Name and honour the losses driving the pattern
4. The Cost Inventory	Acknowledge	Own the full cost — and convert it into agency
5. The Three-Hand Method	All stages	Real-time diagnostic compass for every interaction
6. The Deliberate Step Back	Loosen	Build the neural pathway of deliberate choice through live practice
7. The Evidence File	Loosen onward	Accumulate the personal, irrefutable counter-argument to catastrophising
8. The Open Question Practice	Listen	Build the bridge — ask without managing, listen without redirecting
9. The Repair Conversation	Listen	Acknowledge the pattern to the child, release the outcome completely
10. The Consistency Protocol	Listen onward	Convert insight into a lasting habit through daily, weekly, and monthly practice

Appendix A Table 2: Showing the Complete Toolkit at a Glance

Appendix B: The Science Behind the System

An accessible summary of the four evidence bases underpinning the Love Without Walls System — for the reader whose analytical mind wants the full academic foundation beneath the framework.

Evidence Base 1 — Attachment Theory (Bowlby and Ainsworth)

John Bowlby's foundational work on attachment — developed across his three-volume series *Attachment*, *Separation*, and *Loss* (1969, 1973, 1980) — established the central thesis that the human need for close emotional bonds is not a learned behaviour but a biological imperative. Children are wired from birth to seek proximity to a primary attachment figure as a survival mechanism. The quality of that attachment — determined largely by the consistency, sensitivity, and availability of the parent's responses — shapes the child's internal working model of relationships: their beliefs about whether they are worthy of love and whether other people can be trusted to provide it.

Mary Ainsworth's Strange Situation studies (1978) identified three primary attachment styles — secure, anxious-ambivalent, and avoidant — and showed that securely attached children are characterised by a specific quality of parental behaviour: the parent who is reliably available, genuinely responsive, and, critically, who supports the child's autonomous exploration rather than restricting it out of their own anxiety.

The Love Without Walls System draws directly on this research in its central framework distinction between the Closed Hand (anxious, restricting attachment behaviour) and the Open Hand (secure, exploration-supporting attachment behaviour). The WALLS Framework's progression from Witness to Soar maps directly onto the attachment research's findings about what produces secure attachment in the child and what produces anxious attachment — and what the parent must change in themselves to shift the relationship from the latter to the former.

Key finding for this framework: The securely attached child is not produced by a parent who holds tighter in response to separation anxiety. They are produced by a parent who is reliably present, genuinely responsive, and — particularly during adolescence — willing to support the child's growing autonomy rather than restrict it in the parent's service's own anxiety management.

Evidence Base 2 — Adolescent Neuroscience (Daniel Siegel)

Daniel Siegel's research on the adolescent brain — synthesised in *Brainstorm: The Power and Purpose of the Teenage Brain* (2013) and his broader work on interpersonal neurobiology — provides the neurological foundation for understanding why the Closed Hand parenting approach is counterproductive during adolescence, and why the specific practices of the Loosen and Listen stages are designed the way they are.

Siegel identifies four fundamental drives of the adolescent brain that distinguish it from the adult brain:

Novelty-seeking: The adolescent brain has a heightened drive for new experiences and a reduced sensitivity to dopamine-based rewards that motivate adult behaviour — producing the risk-taking and boundary-testing that the anxious parent experiences as threatening.

Social engagement: The adolescent brain is hyper-attuned to peer relationships and peer evaluation, and hyper-sensitive to social threat — including the specific social threat of a parent who monitors and manages in ways that communicate distrust.

Increased emotional intensity: The adolescent brain produces stronger emotional responses to stimuli than the adult brain, with less effective prefrontal regulation of those responses, which is why the hostile teenager's reactions can feel disproportionate, and why the parent's escalating closed-hand response consistently makes them more intense rather than less.

Creative exploration: The adolescent brain is, above all, in the business of identity construction — building, testing, and refining the autonomous self that will carry the person into adult life. This developmental task is the neurological explanation for why the Closed Hand's message, *"I don't trust you to handle this,"* is experienced by the adolescent brain as a direct threat to its central developmental project.

Siegel's work on interpersonal neurobiology also provides the scientific basis for the Identity Reclamation Practice and the parental modelling section of Chapter 16: the parents' own emotional regulation — the quality of their presence, their capacity to manage their own anxiety through trust rather than control — is transmitted to the child through the resonance of the relationship itself. The parent who models open-handed living is not just offering their child a better relationship. They are, through the mechanism of neurological resonance, contributing to the child's developing capacity to regulate their own emotional responses.

Key finding for this framework: The Closed Hand approach does not work with the adolescent brain — neurologically, mechanically, demonstrably. And the parent who understands the neurological basis for the teenager's responses to monitoring, management, and control has a significantly more compassionate and effective framework for navigating them.

Evidence Base 3 — Self-Determination Theory (Deci and Ryan)

Edward Deci and Richard Ryan's Self-Determination Theory (SDT) — developed across decades of research beginning in the 1970s and summarised most accessibly in *Self-Determination and Intrinsic Motivation in Human Behaviour* (1985) — identifies three fundamental psychological needs that must be met for an individual to experience genuine wellbeing, motivation, and flourishing:

Autonomy: The experience of genuine choice and self-direction in one's own actions.

Competence: The experience of being effective in one's interactions with the environment — of mastering challenges and achieving meaningful outcomes.

Relatedness: The experience of meaningful connection with others — of being genuinely seen, heard, and cared for.

The Closed Hand parenting approach, as the Love Without Walls System defines it, systematically undermines all three needs in the child receiving it:

Autonomy is undermined by every intervention that removes the child's choice — every pre-empted consequence, every managed outcome, every decision redirected toward the parent's preferred result.

Competence is undermined by every intervention that removes the child's opportunity to show their own capability — every problem solved before it could be navigated, every challenge softened before it could be met.

Relatedness is undermined by every interaction in which the child experiences the parent's engagement as monitoring rather than genuine interest — in which the question asked is heard as checking rather than curiosity, and the concern offered is experienced as management rather than care.

SDT research consistently shows that individuals whose autonomy, competence, and relatedness needs are chronically undermined develop lower intrinsic motivation, poorer well-being outcomes, and a reduced capacity for genuine self-regulation — the very outcomes that the anxious parent's Closed Hand approach is most desperately trying to prevent.

The Open Hand practices of the WALLS Framework — the Deliberate Step Back, the Open Question structure, the Consistency Protocol — are each designed, in direct alignment with SDT principles, to meet rather than undermine these three fundamental needs. The Deliberate Step Back meets the competence need by creating the conditions for the child to show their own capability. The Open Question meets the autonomy need by expressing a genuine interest in the child's perspective rather than a preferred answer. The Consistency Protocol meets the relatedness need by building a sustained, reliable, genuine connection that SDT identifies as essential for flourishing.

Key finding for this framework: The fear-driven parent is, with the best of intentions, systematically undermining the three psychological needs that produce the very outcomes they most want for their child. The open-handed approach meets all three —

and in doing so, produces both the child's flourishing and the parent's relationship with a child who is genuinely thriving.

Evidence Base 4 — Cognitive Behavioural Research on Anxiety Regulation

The cognitive behavioural research on anxiety regulation provides the psychological mechanism behind two of the framework's most practically important claims: that anxiety-driven parenting operates faster than conscious thought, and that it can be interrupted and replaced through deliberate, repetition-based practice.

The foundational CBT model — developed by Aaron Beck in the 1960s and extended by subsequent researchers into the specific field of parental anxiety — identifies the cognitive distortions that characterise anxious parenting:

Catastrophising: The systematic overestimation of threat and underestimation of the individual's capacity to cope — the specific distortion that produces the gap between the feared outcome and the actual outcome that the Evidence File documents and counters.

Hypervigilance: The sustained attentional focus on potential threats that produces the constant, low-level scanning behaviour characteristic of the Closed Hand parent — and the physiological depletion that comes with it.

Emotional reasoning: The assumption that because something feels dangerous, it is — the cognitive mechanism that makes the anxiety's threat assessment feel like reality rather than prediction.

The CBT research on anxiety regulation consistently identifies two interventions as most effective in addressing these distortions:

Exposure: Deliberately and gradually encountering the feared stimulus without the avoidance behaviour (the Closed Hand intervention) — the neurological mechanism behind the Deliberate Step Back and the Anxiety Tolerance Reflection. Each exposure that produces a survivable rather than catastrophic outcome weakens the catastrophising distortion by providing counter-evidence that the threat assessment was inaccurate.

Cognitive restructuring: The deliberate identification and challenging of the cognitive distortions — the mechanism behind the Fear Audit's diagnostic question (*"If I were not afraid, would I still do this?"*) and the Evidence File's systematic counter-argument to the catastrophising loop.

The neuroplasticity research that underpins the Three-Hand Method's daily log and the Consistency Protocol provides the biological mechanism for why repetition is the operative principle: the neural pathway of deliberate choice is built through repetition, not insight. The parent who understands this — who knows that the hundredth use of the Three-Second Check is more powerful than the first, not because the check has changed but because the pathway it is building has become more established — has the specific, biological rationale for sustaining the practice through the seasons when its results are invisible.

Key finding for this framework: Anxiety that has been driving parenting behaviour for years cannot be addressed through understanding alone. It requires deliberate, graduated, repetition-based exposure to the feared stimulus — not intervening — combined with the systematic documentation of actual outcomes as counter-evidence to the catastrophising distortion. This is precisely what the Loosen stage's tools produce.

Appendix C: A Glossary of Open-Handed Love

Definitions of the book's core terms and framework language — a portable reference for difficult moments, partner conversations, and therapeutic contexts.

The Closed Hand: The parenting mode driven by unresolved fear and anxiety. Characterised by monitoring, managing, pre-empting, and intervening — behaviours that feel like love from the inside but are experienced as distrust by the child receiving them. The Closed Hand is not a character flaw. It is a conditioned response, built from inherited beliefs about love and safety, that can be replaced through deliberate practice.

The Open Hand: The parenting mode driven by genuine trust. Characterised by allowing, waiting, genuine curiosity, and the tolerance of uncertainty. The Open Hand does not mean disengagement or indifference — it is the active, conscious choice to trust the child's capability and to create the conditions under which that capability can be shown. The central practice of the WALLS Frameworks Loosen and Listen stages.

The Guiding Hand: The parenting mode of invited mentorship. Neither the grip of the Closed Hand nor the complete release of the Open Hand — the Guiding Hand is the appropriately boundaried involvement of a parent who has been asked for their perspective and who offers it without requiring it to be followed. The natural mode of a mature, flourishing parent-child relationship.

The WALLS Framework: The five-stage roadmap of the Love Without Walls System. Each stage is a doorway that opens in sequence, each one creating the conditions that make the next stage possible. The stages are: Witness, Acknowledge, Loosen, Listen, Soar.

Witness (W) The first stage of the WALLS Framework. The deliberate, honest, compassionate self-observation that produces the parent's most accurate map of their own pattern — its daily behaviours, its underlying fears, and the grief operating beneath them. Witnessing is not judgment. It is illumination.

Acknowledge (A) The second stage of the WALLS Framework. The movement from passive recognition to active ownership — feeling the full weight of the pattern's cost and converting that weight, through the distinction between guilt and shame, into the irrevocable internal decision that something is going to change.

Loosen (L — first) The third stage of the WALLS Framework. The most practically demanding stage — the deliberate, graduated, logged practice of releasing the grip in real interactions with real consequences. Built through the Three-Hand Method as a daily operating system, the Deliberate Step Back, and the Evidence File.

Listen (L — second). The fourth stage of the WALLS Framework. The bridge-building stage — the Open Question practice, the Repair Conversation, and the Consistency Protocol that together create the relational conditions under which a child who has been protecting themselves offers a genuine response.

Soar (S) The fifth stage of the WALLS Framework. The identity reclamation and flourishing stage — the deliberate investment in the full self beyond the parenting role, producing the parent whose child finds most worth returning to. Soar is not a destination but a living state requiring ongoing tending.

The Fear Audit: A written self-assessment tool for the Witness stage. Maps the parents' ten most frequent parenting interventions to the underlying fears, applies the Three-Hand classification, and uses the diagnostic question — *"If I were not afraid right now, would I still do this?"* — to separate genuine care from anxiety-driven behaviour.

The Evidence File: The running written record of the Loosen stage. Documents every instance of the child showing capability, resilience, or growth without parental intervention — building the personal, irrefutable counter-argument to the catastrophising loop that drives the Closed Hand.

The Flourish Markers: The specific, emotionally precise indicators that signal the transformation is real — defined by the parent in the Soar stage as the particular moments that matter most to them and to this relationship. Not generic milestones but personal images: the voluntary phone call, the Sunday dinner chosen freely, the actual conversation, the adult friendship freely given. Used as an orientation in hard seasons.

The Legacy Letter: The private, unsealed letter written to the child in the Soar stage — not to be sent, but kept as the clearest possible evidence of who the parent has become, the relationship they are building, and the love they now offer with open hands. Completed in Chapter 18 with a final section written from the other side of the transformation.

The Legacy Vision: The long-view articulation of how the parent wants to be remembered by their child — not in a eulogy, but in the ordinary, specific, day-to-day texture of the relationship the child will carry forward into their own adult life. Distinct from the Legacy Letter in its orientation: the Letter is addressed to the child, the Vision is the parent's own north star.

The Repair Conversation: A three-element framework for initiating an honest, vulnerable, agenda-free conversation about the relationship. Contains only: acknowledgement (*I see what has been happening*), ownership (*I am working on my part in it*), and release (*I am not asking you to respond*). The outcome is released completely and unconditionally.

The Rupture Recovery Tool: The three-step sequence for returning to the framework within twenty-four hours of an old-pattern interaction — without self-flagellation, without shame spiral. Steps: Name It Without Narrative (one sentence, the behaviour only), Identify the Condition (the specific circumstances under which the old pattern fired), The Return Commitment (one specific, achievable forward action).

Guilt versus Shame: The distinction that underpins the entire book's approach to self-compassion and change. Guilt says: *I did something that needs to change* — it points forward and is productive fuel. Shame says: *I am something that cannot change* — it collapses inward and is paralysing. The Cost Inventory and the Acknowledge stage produce guilt in its productive form while actively dismantling shame.

The Catastrophising Loop: The cognitive pattern, underpinned by the anxiety distortion of catastrophising, that systematically overestimates threat and underestimates the child's capacity to cope. Addressed directly by the Evidence File (counter-evidence), the Deliberate Step Back (graduated exposure), and the Three-Question Reflection (the gap between feared and actual outcomes).

The Consistency Protocol: The daily, weekly, and monthly practice structure of the Listen stage that converts insight into lasting habits. Daily five-minute check-ins. Weekly twenty-minute review. Monthly sixty-minute WALLS assessment. Maintained through every season — the rewarding and the difficult equally — because consistency in the absence of visible reward is the single most powerful signal to a watching child that this time is different.

This concludes Love With Open Hands: The One Shift That Turns the Most Strained Parent-Child Relationship Into Both of You Choose.

The toolkit is yours. The map is in your hands. The compass is in your pocket.

And the love you are offering — with open hands, with clear eyes, with the courage it took to get here — is the love that will last.

Chapter Twenty-One

References

The following references are organised by the four evidence bases underpinning The Love Without Walls System.

Attachment Theory

Bowlby and Ainsworth

Ainsworth, M. D. S., Blehar, M. C., Waters, E., & Wall, S. (1978). *Patterns of attachment: A psychological study of the strange situation*. Lawrence Erlbaum Associates.

Ainsworth, M. D. S. (1963). The development of infant-mother interaction among the Ganda. In B. M. Foss (Ed.), *Determinants of infant behaviour* (Vol. 2, pp. 67–112). Methuen.

Ainsworth, M. D. S. (1982). Attachment: Retrospect and prospect. In C. M. Parkes & J. Stevenson-Hinde (Eds.), *The place of attachment in human behaviour* (pp. 3–30). Basic Books.

Ainsworth, M. D. S., & Bowlby, J. (1991). An ethological approach to personality development. *American Psychologist, 46*(4), 333–341. https://doi.org/10.1037/0003-066X.46.4.333

Bowlby, J. (1944). Forty-four juvenile thieves: Their characters and home-life. *International Journal of Psycho-Analysis, 25*, 19–53.

Bowlby, J. (1951). *Maternal care and mental health*. World Health Organization.

Bowlby, J. (1969). *Attachment and loss: Vol. 1. Attachment*. Basic Books.

Bowlby, J. (1973). *Attachment and loss: Vol. 2. Separation: Anxiety and anger*. Basic Books.

Bowlby, J. (1980). *Attachment and loss: Vol. 3. Loss: Sadness and depression*. Basic Books.

Bowlby, J. (1982). *Attachment and loss: Vol. 1. Attachment* (2nd ed.). Basic Books. (Original work published 1969)

Bowlby, J. (1988). *A secure base: Parent-child attachment and healthy human development*. Basic Books.

Bretherton, I. (1992). The origins of attachment theory: John Bowlby and Mary Ainsworth. *Developmental Psychology, 28*(5), 759–775. https://doi.org/10.1037/0012-1649.28.5.759

Cassidy, J., & Shaver, P. R. (Eds.). (2008). *Handbook of attachment: Theory, research, and clinical applications* (2nd ed.). Guilford Press.

Main, M., Kaplan, N., & Cassidy, J. (1985). Security in infancy, childhood, and adulthood: A move to the level of representation. *Monographs of the Society for Research in Child Development, 50*(1–2), 66–104. https://doi.org/10.2307/3333827

Adolescent Neuroscience

Daniel J. Siegel

Siegel, D. J. (2001). *The developing mind: How relationships and the brain interact to shape who we are*. Guilford Press.

Siegel, D. J. (2010). *Mindsight: The new science of personal transformation*. Bantam Books.

Siegel, D. J. (2013). *Brainstorm: The power and purpose of the teenage brain*. Jeremy P. Tarcher/Penguin.

Siegel, D. J., & Hartzell, M. (2003). *Parenting from the inside out: How a deeper self-understanding can help you raise children who thrive*. Jeremy P. Tarcher/Penguin.

Siegel, D. J., & Bryson, T. P. (2011). *The whole-brain child: 12 revolutionary strategies to nurture your child's developing mind*. Delacorte Press.

Siegel, D. J., & Bryson, T. P. (2020). *The power of showing up: How parental presence shapes who our kids become and how their brains get wired*. Ballantine Books.

Self-Determination Theory

Deci and Ryan

Deci, E. L., & Ryan, R. M. (1985). *Intrinsic motivation and self-determination in human behavior*. Plenum.

Deci, E. L., & Ryan, R. M. (2000). The "what" and "why" of goal pursuits: Human needs and the self-determination of behavior. *Psychological Inquiry*, *11*(4), 227–268. https://doi.org/10.1207/S15327965PLI1104_01

Grolnick, W. S., & Ryan, R. M. (1989). Parent styles associated with children's self-regulation and competence in school. *Journal of Educational Psychology*, *81*(2), 143–154. https://doi.org/10.1037/0022-0663.81.2.143

Grolnick, W. S., Ryan, R. M., & Deci, E. L. (1991). Inner resources for school achievement: Motivational mediators of children's perceptions of their parents. *Journal of Educational Psychology*, *83*(4), 508–517. https://doi.org/10.1037/0022-0663.83.4.508

Ryan, R. M., & Deci, E. L. (2000). Self-determination theory and the facilitation of intrinsic motivation, social development, and well-being. *American Psychologist*, *55*(1), 68–78. https://doi.org/10.1037/0003-066X.55.1.68

Ryan, R. M., & Deci, E. L. (2017). *Self-determination theory: Basic psychological needs in motivation, development, and wellness*. Guilford Press.

Soenens, B., & Vansteenkiste, M. (2010). A theoretical upgrade of the concept of parental psychological control: Proposing new insights based on self-determination theory. *Developmental Review*, *30*(1), 74–99. https://doi.org/10.1016/j.dr.2009.11.001

Cognitive Behavioural Research

Anxiety Regulation

Beck, A. T. (1976). *Cognitive therapy and emotional disorders*. International Universities Press.

Beck, A. T., Rush, A. J., Shaw, B. F., & Emery, G. (1979). *Cognitive therapy of depression*. Guilford Press.

Beck, A. T., Emery, G., & Greenberg, R. L. (1985). *Anxiety disorders and phobias: A cognitive perspective*. Basic Books.

Beck, J. S. (1995). *Cognitive therapy: Basics and beyond*. Guilford Press.

Clark, D. M., & Beck, A. T. (1988). Cognitive approaches. In C. G. Last & M. Hersen (Eds.), *Handbook of anxiety disorders* (pp. 362–385). Pergamon.

Craske, M. G., & Barlow, D. H. (2008). Panic disorder and agoraphobia. In D. H. Barlow (Ed.), *Clinical handbook of psychological disorders: A step-by-step treatment manual* (4th ed., pp. 1–64). Guilford Press.

Foa, E. B., & Kozak, M. J. (1986). Emotional processing of fear: Exposure to corrective information. *Psychological Bulletin, 99*(1), 20–35. https://doi.org/10.1037/0033-2909.99.1.20

Salkovskis, P. M. (1991). The importance of behaviour in the maintenance of anxiety and panic: A cognitive account. *Behavioural Psychotherapy, 19*(1), 6–19. https://doi.org/10.1017/S0141347300011472

Chapter Twenty-Two

Reader Review Requests

1. <u>Amazon Review Request:</u>

A Personal Note on Reviews

If this book has made a difference to you — or to the relationship you were trying to find your way back to — I want to ask you something.

Not for five stars. Not for a polished testimonial. Just for the truth of your experience, written in your own words, in the place where another parent will find it at 11 pm when they need to know whether this book is worth opening.

That parent is real. They are sitting somewhere right now with the same combination of love and fear and exhaustion that brought you to these pages. And the most useful thing they will read before they decide whether to begin this journey is not a description of the book.

It is the honest account of a parent who has already taken it.

If you are willing — and only if you are willing — a review on Amazon takes less than five minutes and has the specific, practical effect of putting this book in front of the parent who needs it most, at the moment they need it most.

You can leave your review here: **[Amazon review link]**

It does not need to be long. It does not need to be polished. It just needs to be true.

Thank you — for reading, for doing the work, and for the love that brought you this far.

2. <u>Multi-Source Review Request.:</u>

Would You Help Another Parent Find This Book?

If *Love With Open Hands* has been part of your journey — if something in these pages helped you see your pattern more clearly, name a grief you hadn't found words for, or take the first deliberate step toward the relationship you were building toward — I would be genuinely grateful for your help.

Not a performance. Not a polished recommendation. Just your honest experience, shared in a place where another parent might find it.

Here are the places where a review or a rating makes the most difference:

Amazon: The single highest-impact place to leave a review. Even two or three sentences from a real reader change the way the book surfaces for parents who are searching at their most vulnerable moments. → [https://www.amazon.com/dp/B0GX2XYPJP]

Scan me

Goodreads: For readers who trust book communities over algorithms — a Goodreads rating or review reaches a specific, engaged audience of people who take their reading seriously. → [Goodreads link]

Your own community: A personal recommendation — in a parenting group, a private message to a friend you know is struggling, a post in a Facebook group where parents are honest about the hard parts — reaches the exact person this book was written for. You do not need an audience to make a difference. You need one person who needs to hear that there is a map.

A note to therapists, coaches, and practitioners If you work with parents navigating this terrain and have found this book useful in your practice, a professional review or recommendation — on your website, in your newsletter, or through your professional networks — carries a specific weight that reaches people in the exact moment they are seeking support.

What to Write?

If you are not sure what to say, here are the only three questions worth answering:

Where were you when you found this book? Not your life history — just the emotional location. The thing that brought you here.

What shifted? Not what you learned — what changed in how you saw yourself, your child, or the relationship between you.

Who would you give this book to? The specific parent you would put it in front of if you could.

Your answers to those three questions, written honestly and in your own words, is everything another parent needs to decide whether to begin.

Thank you for reading. Thank you for the work you have done. And thank you, genuinely, for being willing to pass it forward.

Love With Open Hands: The One Shift That Turns the Most Strained Parent-Child Relationship Into One *Both of You Choose*